T0360611

Neuroscience and Entrepreneurship Research

This book asserts the emergence of the fourth era of entrepreneurship, based on a brain-driven approach to the study, instruction, and practice of entrepreneurship. This paradigm shift stems from the need to incorporate appropriate neurotechnologies into the exploration and enhancement of entrepreneurial phenomena in order to best address the field's methodological challenges. The author explains why a paradigm shift is necessary in the field of entrepreneurship and provides the foundational guidelines for those interested in implementing it. Furthermore, a model of entrepreneurial enhancement is conceptualized and signalled as the ultimate goal of this new era. Scholars, practitioners, policymakers, and students interested in advancing entrepreneurship's contribution to academia, business, and society at large will benefit from this new era's multidisciplinary perspective and unique strengths.

Víctor Pérez Centeno is Founder, Brain-driven Entrepreneurship Expert, Researcher, and Educator at WNYLE Entrepreneurship Institute, Finland.

Routledge Focus on Business and Management

The fields of business and management have grown exponentially as areas of research and education. This growth presents challenges for readers trying to keep up with the latest important insights. *Routledge Focus on Business and Management* presents small books on big topics and how they intersect with the world of business research.

Individually, each title in the series provides coverage of a key academic topic, whilst collectively, the series forms a comprehensive collection across the business disciplines.

Risk Management Maturity
A Multidimensional Model
Sylwia Bąk and Piotr Jedynak

Proposal Writing for Business Research Projects
Peter Samuels

Systems Thinking and Sustainable Healthcare Delivery
Ben Fong

Gender Diversity and Inclusion at Work
Divergent Views from Turkey
Zeynep Özsoy, Mustafa Şenyücel and Beyza Oba

Management and Visualisation
Seeing Beyond the Strategic
Gordon Fletcher

For more information about this series, please visit: www.routledge.com/ Routledge-Focus-on-Business-and-Management/book-series/FBM

Neuroscience and Entrepreneurship Research

Researching Brain-Driven Entrepreneurship

Víctor Pérez Centeno

Routledge
Taylor & Francis Group

NEW YORK AND LONDON

First published 2023
by Routledge
605 Third Avenue, New York, NY 10158

and by Routledge
4 Park Square, Milton Park, Abingdon, Oxon, OX14 4RN

Routledge is an imprint of the Taylor & Francis Group, an informa business

Library of Congress Cataloging-in-Publication Data
Names: Pérez Centeno, Víctor, author.
Title: Neuroscience and entrepreneurship research : researching brain-driven
    entrepreneurship / Víctor Pérez Centeno.
Description: New York, NY : Routledge, 2023. | Series: Routledge focus on
    business and management | Includes bibliographical references and index.
Identifiers: LCCN 2022044093 | ISBN 9780367480615 (hardback) |
    ISBN 9780367522407 (paperback) | ISBN 9781003057109 (ebook)
Subjects: LCSH: Entrepreneurship—Research. | Neurosciences—Research.
Classification: LCC HB615 .P39329 2023 | DDC 658.4/21072—dc23/eng/
    20221123
LC record available at https://lccn.loc.gov/2022044093

ISBN: 978-0-367-48061-5 (hbk)
ISBN: 978-0-367-52240-7 (pbk)
ISBN: 978-1-003-05710-9 (ebk)

DOI: 10.4324/9781003057109

Typeset in Times New Roman
by Apex CoVantage, LLC

Contents

Abbreviations

ADHD	Attention deficit hyperactivity disorder
BRE	Brain-driven entrepreneurship
BT	Brain training
EEG	Electroencephalography
ERP	Event-related potentials
fMRI	Functional magnetic image resonance
MEG	Magnetoencephalography
tDCS	Transcranial direct current stimulation
TMS	Transcranial magnetic stimulation
NIRS	Near infrared spectroscopy
NF	Neurofeedback
EPN	Early posterior negativity
LPP	Late positive potential
LPC	Late positive complex
N100	A negative deflection peaking between 90 and 200 ms after the onset of the stimulus, is observed when an unexpected stimulus is presented.
N400	It is a negative wave first described in the context of semantic incongruity, 300–600 ms post-stimulus.

Preface

My desire for this book stemmed from my realization that for decades, the study, teaching, and practice of entrepreneurship had become stale. As the world strives for greater efficiency and well-being, I believe that the field of entrepreneurship must rise to the occasion. This book is intended to demonstrate that a brain-driven approach to entrepreneurship is the new paradigm for entrepreneurship and has the potential to add value to society. The book's six parts provide the elements required to facilitate the transition from a traditional to a brain-driven research paradigm.

The first section describes the three previous stages of the evolution of entrepreneurship throughout history. It sets the stage for me to introduce what I call the fourth era of entrepreneurship, the brain era, where I believe the discipline of entrepreneurship is headed. The second section conceptualizes and develops the brain-driven approach to entrepreneurship, along with its two major components: neurotechnologies and experimental design. In this part, I also introduce the concept of 'entrepreneurial enhancement' and position it as the ultimate goal of the brain-driven era of entrepreneurship. The third part focuses on seven relevant entrepreneurship topics that could benefit greatly from a brain-driven research approach. The fourth section looks to the future of the field by developing a set of appropriate neurotechnologies and approaches for assessing, stimulating, and enhancing entrepreneurial performance. The fifth part discusses the key implications and disruptions that I believe neurotechnologies will bring to the discipline. In the sixth section, I discuss my proposed research agenda for the near future, as well as my concluding thoughts on the enormous opportunities that the brain era opens up for a wide range of actors involved in the fascinating world of entrepreneurship. It is time to look at entrepreneurship from the inside out: the brain.

Part I

The past and present of entrepreneurship

1 Introduction

The brain is increasingly becoming the centre of interest in the race to improve human performance. To gain a competitive advantage in the exploration of the human brain using neuroscience, the United States, and continental organizations such as the European Union have launched large-scale initiatives such as the White House BRAIN Initiative and the Human Brain Project (EU).

While the use of neuroscience has spread rapidly in disciplines such as marketing, education, management, and leadership, it has not spread as quickly or as intensely in the realm of entrepreneurship.

Only a small number of entrepreneurship scholars have recognized the significance of neuroscience in the field (de Holan, 2014; Krueger & Welpe, 2014; Pérez-Centeno, 2017; Shane, Drover, Clingingsmith, & Cerf, 2020) and some isolated research and application-driven initiatives have emerged. For example, the King's College London Neuroscience of Entrepreneurship Project, the WNYLE Institute's Entrepreneurial Brain Educational Programme, and the Copenhagen Business School's Entrepreneurs' Cognition and Perception of Risk and Ambiguity project.

But, beyond the contribution of neurotechnologies, there is a more profound issue at stake: the need to introduce a new era within the discipline that repositions the entrepreneur's brain as the epicentre of academic concern,

The benefits are unique, as stated in this book, but there is a challenge to overcome; entrepreneurship scholars are trained to deal with data collected through traditional research methods such as surveys, interviews, and case studies (McDonald, Gan, Fraser, Oke, & Anderson, 2015), they are, however, less familiar with the collection and evaluation of objective data from the entrepreneur's brain, let alone using this evidence to develop new mechanisms to enhance the entrepreneur's knowledge acquisition, information processing, and reasoning abilities (Kiely, 2014).

Unlike the three preceding eras discussed in the following section, the fourth era of entrepreneurship presented in this book contends that a

DOI: 10.4324/9781003057109-2

brain-driven perspective is required to overcome the field's current technological and methodological limitations in order to best understand and improve the performance and health of the entrepreneurial brain.

The book is written for a wide range of readers, but it is primarily aimed at academics, students, policymakers, entrepreneurship instructors, and entrepreneurs interested in novel paths to examine and boost entrepreneurial success. It is a research-based source of knowledge that can be applied to any type and level of entrepreneurship course.

2 The three preceding eras

Over the course of its history, entrepreneurship as a research field (Lohrke & Landström, 2010) has mainly undergone on three stages of Darwinian evolution. An earlier 'economic' interest in dissecting what happens in the market when an entrepreneur acts (1870–1940) (Landström, 2007); a 'social/psychological' orientation to investigate who the entrepreneur is and why entrepreneurs act in certain ways (1940–1970); and finally a 'managerial' perspective concerned with evaluating entrepreneurship as a process (1940–1970) (Landström, 2004).

The developments attained during these stages helped laying the theoretical groundwork of the field, however, it still faces methodological and technological limitations that require a new approach. These difficulties have become more apparent in entrepreneurial cognition research, because it deals with the intriguing question of how entrepreneurs think (Mitchell et al., 2007).

Prior research on entrepreneurial cognition (Brush, Manolova, & Edelman, 2008; Jack, 2010) reveals the dominance of positivistic approaches and data gathering methods such as surveys, case studies, and interviews. Positivism emphasizes the significance of the relationship between the variables being studied and the results of those studies (McDonald et al., 2015). Methodological issues arise because of the difficulty in reflecting on one's own conscious processes when using these approaches (Omorede, Thorgren, & Wincent, 2015).

One of the major drawbacks of conventional methods utilized in prior eras of entrepreneurship research is that they do not allow the collection and analysis of data directly from the entrepreneur's brain (Pérez-Centeno, 2017). In so doing, the obtention of higher quality data which could lead to a better assessment of a particular phenomenon is drastically reduced.

The mitigation of these limitations calls for the emergence of a new era, one that embraces a new and more efficient approach for the investigation of entrepreneurial behaviour. It is sustained that in this new era the

DOI: 10.4324/9781003057109-3

entrepreneur's brain should be the new protagonist and neurotechnologies should be welcomed as the most fitting tools to explore entrepreneur's brain.

Neurotechnologies can help to reduce current limitations because their experimental nature can boost theory building (Kraus, Meier, & Niemand, 2016), which is desperately needed in the field. More importantly, neurotechnologies can be used to best explore new mechanisms for improving entrepreneurial performance. The latter is a distinct advantage of the fourth era of entrepreneurship, which is discussed in the following section.

The realization of scholars about the importance of incorporating neuroscience technologies into their work is one of the first signs of the brain era in entrepreneurship (Blair, 2010; de Holan, 2014; McMullen, Wood, & Palich, 2014; Nicolaou & Shane, 2014; Pérez-Centeno, 2017).

However, as detailed in the following section, the fourth era transcends the incorporation of neurotechnologies; it is a paradigm shift aimed at re-engineering the way entrepreneurship is studied, taught, and practiced from an entirely new perspective: the entrepreneurs' brains. Figure 1 depicts the brain-driven era in the evolution of entrepreneurship research.

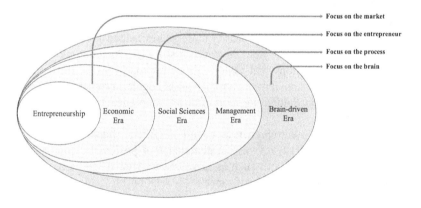

Figure 1 Evolution of entrepreneurship research and the new brain-driven era

Source: own elaboration

Part II

The brain-driven era

3 The fourth era

This section examines the central concept of the fourth era of entrepreneurship, which emphasizes the adoption of a brain-driven perspective for optimally evaluating entrepreneurial behaviour and improving entrepreneurial performance in terms of greater and healthier entrepreneurial success.

3.1 Defining the brain-driven approach to entrepreneurship

In layman's terms, a brain-driven approach to entrepreneurship can be defined as 'the investigation of an entrepreneurship issue and the enhancement of a specific entrepreneurial skill, which may be cognitive, affective, or conative in nature, using an appropriate neuroscience technology'. For example, from a cognitive standpoint, it is more about evaluating how entrepreneurs think than what entrepreneurs are, have, or do (de Holan, 2014).

A brain-driven research approach should not necessarily be equalized with concepts such as neuro-entrepreneurship (also known as entrepreneurial neuroscience) and experimental entrepreneurship. Experimental entrepreneurship, focuses on the use of experiments to investigate entrepreneurial behaviour, whereas neuro-entrepreneurship concentrates on the investigation of entrepreneurial behaviour using methods associated with cognitive neuroscience (Krueger & Welpe, 2014).

3.2 Advantages of a brain-driven approach

The brain era implies the ability to use neurotechnologies to capture and assess what happens in the brain of the entrepreneur without the need for questions, thereby avoiding issues of confusion, desirability, or outright lies (Cela-Conde et al., 2004). Instead of focusing on the verbalization of thought to determine what is happening in the mind, neurotechnologies examine the mind itself while it is performing a task (de Holan, 2014).

DOI: 10.4324/9781003057109-5

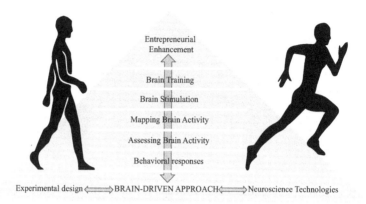

Figure 2 Strengths of a brain-driven approach to entrepreneurship research, education, and practise.

Source: own elaboration

Fitting neurotechnologies have the potential to better investigate (Krueger & Welpe, 2014) (McMullen et al., 2014; Nicolaou & Shane, 2014), and to test how entrepreneurs think (Krueger & Welpe, 2008; Smith, 2010; Wargo, Baglini, & Nelson, 2010), how entrepreneurs perceive and act on opportunities, what areas of their brain are activated when they do so, and whether these differences exist between entrepreneurs and non-entrepreneurs (de Holan, 2014).

The value of a brain-driven approach to the discipline of entrepreneurship, as discussed further in the following chapters, may result in an in-depth examination of topics that cannot be approached using traditional methods, the opportunity to boost theory development, the generation of brain-driven data used for the localization of relevant cognitive processes and the ability to stimulate key executive functions linked to entrepreneurial success. It goes without saying that it has the potential to spark the development of novel brain-training protocols to enhance entrepreneurial performance.

As implied by Krueger and Welpe (2014), a brain-driven approach to the study and practice of entrepreneurship entails the ability to ask questions that have never been answered and to test questions that have never been considered to be asked. If we are to advance our understanding of entrepreneurial behaviour, we cannot afford to ignore the genesis of any decision and action: the brain.

Figure 2 summarizes the advantages of a brain-driven approach to entrepreneurship research, education and practice.

3.3 Apparent limitations of neurotechnologies

A new paradigm takes time to spread in any field, including entrepreneurship. The need to foster synergies between neuroscience and entrepreneurship, as asserted in this book, is met with natural scepticism (Beugré, 2010). It is contended that cognitive processes are difficult to investigate using neurotechnologies because previous findings have been unimpressive, mixed, muddled, and relatively true (McBride, 2015; Tracey & Schluppeck, 2014). This way of thinking is relative.

There are essentially two limitations to using neurotechnologies, which we believe should be viewed as natural stages of refinement of a particular approach rather than fixed constraints. First, the reliance of functional neuroimaging techniques on the so called 'reverse inference', by which the engagement of a particular cognitive process is inferred from the activation of a particular brain region (Poldrack, 2006, 2011; Rolls & Treves, 2011).

For example, just because a part of the brain appears to be active while a person is performing a task does not necessarily imply that this is the part of the brain in charge of that task (Logothetis, 2008).

Second, in accordance with the first constraint, it is claimed that neurotechnologies such as fMRI produce correlative measures of brain activity, making it difficult to investigate the causal role of specific brain activations in a chosen behaviour (Glimcher, Camerer, Fehr, & Poldrack, 2009). For instance, a statistical correlation between fMRI data and task performance does not imply that the spotted areas indicate a causal relationship (Tracey & Schluppeck, 2014).

Even though it is difficult to claim that a specific cognitive function can be limited to a small section of the brain (Tracey & Schluppeck, 2014), it should be noted in both cases that neuroimaging techniques do not represent the entirety of neurotechnologies. There are neurotechnologies that deal with assessment issues like EEG and brain function enhancement like tDCS and neurofeedback that are not always related to reverse inference.

Aside from the difficulties associated with reverse inference in brain-activation research, we believe that the true potential of the brain-driven paradigm in entrepreneurship lies in the articulated use of proper neurotechnologies and experimentation, the two engines of the brain's era, to assess, develop, and strengthen the cognitive, affective, and conative functions of the entrepreneur's brain. The alleged constraints would not necessarily apply to this latter goal.

4 The two engines of the brain's era

Neuroscientists study the functions of the human brain (Kandel, Schwartz, & Jessell, 2000), whereas entrepreneurship scholars study the entrepreneurial act (Bruyat & Julien, 2001). In both cases, the brain is the source of behaviour. This section explains the fundamentals of the two pillars of a brain-driven approach to entrepreneurship: a set of appropriate neurotechnologies and laboratory experimentation.

Neuroscience devices have advanced so quickly in terms of temporal and spatial resolution that scientific researchers now have hundreds of tools at their disposal to investigate how the nervous system develops over time, its structure, and what it does (Nordqvist, 2014).

These technologies are regarded as the next thorough source of competitive advantage for entrepreneurs because they could not only help to achieve more accurate analysis of entrepreneurship but also help to accelerate entrepreneurs' performance for successful business creation.

There are countless neuroscience technologies available for human use (Bunge & Kahn, 2009), and they can address various facets of neural function such as neuronal firing, brain metabolism, and neurotransmitter levels (Ruff & Huettel, 2014). More specifically, these technologies can ascertain a variety of neural structures active during certain mental operations (Carter & Shieh, 2015) and investigate the brain mechanisms that underpin them (Bunge & Kahn, 2009).

Neuroscience techniques obtain data at multiple levels of the brain and can be classified as invasive or non-invasive. Invasive methods use recordings made with electrodes surgically implanted on the surface or within the depths of the brain, whereas non-invasive techniques record cortical activity using electrodes placed around the head (Alain & Winkler, 2012).

These technologies are classified into four types: methods for monitoring brain electrical activity, methods for indirectly measuring neuronal activity, techniques for modulating brain activity, and optical imaging techniques.

DOI: 10.4324/9781003057109-6

The first type includes EEG and MEG (Bunge & Kahn, 2009), which are known as electromagnetic recording methods (Banich & Compton, 2011).

The methods for measuring neuronal activity work on the assumption that increased local blood flow and metabolic activity support neural activity (Bunge & Kahn, 2009). This category includes fMRI and Positron emission tomography (PET). These devices generate images of physiological processes that highlight neural activation. fMRI and MEG are known as functional imaging techniques (Carter & Shieh, 2015).

TMS, tDCS, and neurofeedback are examples of 'brain stimulation' or 'neuromodulation' techniques used to influence brain activity (Banich & Compton, 2011; Lewis, Thomson, Rosenfeld, & Fitzgerald, 2016). It is been argued that these methods could help to improve attention, memory, and cognitive abilities (Carter & Shieh, 2015).

Optical imaging techniques generate images of neural activity by detecting changes in blood flow and metabolism at the brain's surface (Carter & Shieh, 2015). Optical imaging is an invasive method because it exposes the brain surface to enable light to penetrate and reflect back to a camera; however, near-infrared spectroscopy (NIRS), another method within this classification, is a non-invasive optical imaging alternative that permits the recording of light reflectance through the scalp (Carter & Shieh, 2015).

Functional brain imaging methods are also referred to as 'measurement techniques' because they measure changes in brain function while a research participant engages in some cognitive activity, whereas neuromodulation methods are referred to as 'manipulation techniques' (Ruff & Huettel, 2014) or 'stimulation techniques' (Charron, Fuchs, & Oullier, 2008) because they investigate how perturbations in brain function affect cognitive functions or behaviour (Ruff & Huettel, 2014).

4.1 Appropriate technologies

The use of neuroscience technologies can advance entrepreneurship research; but to do so, one must be familiar with the benefits and drawbacks of each of these tools. Not all techniques can be applied indistinguishably to a specific research theme. Furthermore, in addition to the benefits associated with functional localization, the brain-driven approach claims that neuroscience tools can go a step further: they can enhance entrepreneurial performance.

This assertion gives rise to two new concepts: entrepreneurial enhancement and entrepreneurial performance. Entrepreneurial enhancement is defined as 'the progressive improvement of cognitive, affective, and conative skills in potential or existing entrepreneurs using appropriate neurotechnologies'. Entrepreneurial performance, on the other hand, is defined as

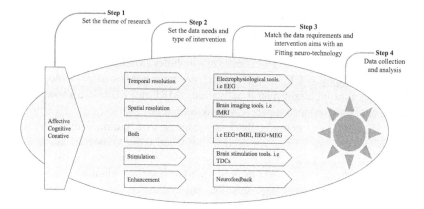

Figure 3 Conceptual model for the examination and enhancement of entrepreneurial behaviour.

Source: own elaboration

'the tangible manifestation and influence of a higher cognitive, affective, or conative capacity in the successful creation of a business'. We argue in this book that 'entrepreneurial enhancement' and 'entrepreneurial performance' are two of the most important contributions that neurotechnologies can make to the field of entrepreneurship.

There are six neuroscience technologies suited to collecting and analysing data from an entrepreneur's brain. These are EEG, MEG, fMRI, TMS, tDCS, and neurofeedback.

However, the use and prowess of each of these techniques necessitates separate expertise, as well as a learning curve to overcome. This is the major entry barrier for entrepreneurship researchers eager to join this camp. It might be hard but not impossible.

Implementing a brain-driven approach necessitates an understanding of the type of data required ahead of time, as well as the type of intervention desired. Figure 3 depicts the conceptual model for the examination and enhancement of entrepreneurial behaviour.

4.2 Experimental design

The second pillar of the entrepreneurs' brain era is experimental design. An experimental design entails conducting an experiment to test a research hypothesis (Huettel, Song, & McCarthy, 2009).

In general, an experiment quantifies the effects of variables of interest on a given behaviour (Charron et al., 2008). Experiments can provide the most reliable and valid analysis of individual behaviour (Patel & Fiet, 2010).

Experiments are regarded as the most robust of all research designs because they allow for the controlled examination of a causal correlational relationship (Coolican, 2014).

Among the four types of experiments that exist: laboratory experiments, quasi-experiments, field experiments, and natural experiments, laboratory experiments are those that are carried out under strictest controlled conditions, allowing for precise measurements. This is the type of experimental approach that is appropriate for the brain era.

Experiments are critical in entrepreneurship because they can establish causality in a relatively unambiguous manner and stringently test a theory (Colquitt, 2008). Moreover, experiments address a fundamental flaw in the field which is the internal validity problem (Krueger & Welpe, 2014). Needles to mention that experiments are an adequate solution when resource constraints prevent a longitudinal study in real-world settings (Davidsson, 2007).

Even though experiments are said to be valuable in entrepreneurship research (Burmeister & Schade, 2007; Hsu, Simmons, & Wieland, 2017; Shepherd & Patzelt, 2015), the use of experimental methodologies in entrepreneurship has received little attention, is limited, uncommon, and insufficient (Aguinis & Lawal, 2012; Hsu et al., 2017; Kraus et al., 2016; Krueger & Welpe, 2008; Patel & Fiet, 2010; Schade & Burmeister, 2009).

For example, entrepreneurship journals rarely publish more than two experimental studies per year (Williams, Wood, Mitchell, & Urbig, 2019). The fact that entrepreneurship is less and less seen as a dualistic individual disposition and more as a result of the interaction between a person, a task, and the environment (Shane, 2003) cements the need for an experimental approach to the field, simply because experiments can manipulate the aforementioned issues with brilliance (Davidsson, 2007).

The relevant point here is that the use of experiments should be prioritized not only because they can add theory-building value (Davidsson, 2007), but also because laboratory experiments, in particular, are inextricably linked to the use of neuroscience technologies, both of which must be used for the brain era to thrive. Another barrier to be mentioned is the scholars' lack of experience with experimental methods.

These issues are natural challenges that arise during paradigm shifts in academia, and entrepreneurship should not be an exception.

4.3 Laboratory experimental design

As explicated in the prior section, the research design that is best aligned with a brain-driven approach is laboratory experimentation.

Laboratory experiments are critical in an entrepreneur's brain era because they allow for the meticulously planning of the design, collection, and analysis of brain-driven data. Experiments as a gold standard against which all other designs are judged (Trochim, 2001) are the best approach to consider. Among the various kinds of experiments, laboratory experiments are the only plausible design to be used in an entrepreneurship brain era because they can produce high internal validity, which can facilitate the generation of new theories that are highly needed in the field nowadays (Hsu et al., 2017). In addition, the high internal validity afforded by these kinds of experiments may mitigate the prevalence of correlational studies with low internal validity due to factors such as self-reporting and retrospective biases (Hsu et al., 2017).

Further to that, laboratory experiments facilitate a more compact control of variables, establish a cause-and-effect relationship, are easier to replicate, and are typically more cost-effective and time-consuming.

Some of the major drawbacks of laboratory experiments include demand characteristics, low realism, low ecological validity, and experimenter bias. However, their upsides outweigh their drawbacks because, unlike field and natural experiments, laboratory experiments are the only design compatible with the use of neuroscience equipment such as MEG and fMRI.

Because the use of laboratory experiments is limited (Hsu et al., 2017) and unstandardized in entrepreneurship research, this section introduces a framework to guide the implementation of an experimental design when combined with a neuroscience technology.

These principles are organized in a logical order and correspond to the stages of laboratory experimentation. The design of the experiment, identification of the independent variable, measurement of the dependent variable, and implementation of a post-experimental follow-up are all part of laboratory experimentation (Wilson, Aronson, & Carlsmith, 2010).

By the end of this section, it should be clear that the main goal of the brain era, 'entrepreneurial enhancement', necessitates the combined forces of neuroscience technologies and laboratory experimentation.

4.4 The nine principles of laboratory experimentation

The four stages of laboratory experimentation are setting the stage of the experiment, constructing the independent variable, measuring the dependent variable, and planning the post-experimental follow-up (Wilson et al., 2010). There are nine principles that depict the most prominent issues to consider when designing a laboratory experiment.

Principle 1: it is all about 'internal validity at first'

Implementing a brain-driven approach entails aiming for high internal validity through laboratory experimentation. Internal validity fosters theory development, which is critical in the field of entrepreneurship.

Internal validity is produced by laboratory experiments because they investigate causality in a controlled environment (Shaver, 2014). Laboratory experiments are particularly useful because they address two significant issues in entrepreneurship research: the inability to rule out alternative explanations and establish causal relationships among variables. Observational studies, self-reports, and correlational analyses, for example, do not usually establish causality because the variables are measured concurrently. As a result, the presence of a significant correlation does not imply that one variable influences another (Hsu et al., 2017).

On the contrary, laboratory experiments test causality, which results in high internal validity when done correctly. A high internal validity fosters new theoretical insights, which are required to strengthen the entrepreneurship foundations (Hsu et al., 2017).

Testing causality in theoretical contributions is important because it can validate or reject theoretically predicted relationships. In other words, a controlled experiment can establish causality (Hsu et al., 2017). If the experiment fails to demonstrate a significant treatment effect, the researcher may revise the design and test different conditions or alternative factors, as well as refine the leading hypothesis (Aronson, Carlsmith, & Ellsworth, 1990).

Laboratory experiments known also as controlled experiments are the ideal tool for testing causality in entrepreneurship research, because once a theory and a causal relationship have been established, the results can be generalized to the real world using other methods (Mook, 1983) such as field and natural experiments.

Field and natural experiments are concerned with generalizing a theory, such as determining whether a theory-predicted relationship would occur in different contexts and answering who, where, and when questions (Hsu et al., 2017). Their greater ecological validity, or the extent to which a study can be generalized to real life, is their strength (Crano, Brewer, & Lac, 2014). Field and natural experiments, however, have lower internal validity than laboratory experiments. As previously stated, it is first and foremost a matter of internal validity.

Because most neurotechnologies are not portable, EEG is the only tool that could potentially be used in laboratory experiments due to its portability.

Principle 2: there is no substitute for accurate data

Though the use of neuroscience techniques has many advantages for entrepreneurship, none of these techniques or signal-processing methods can change the outcome of a poorly designed experiment.

A well-designed experiment necessitates the highest level of data collection accuracy, as failure to do so may jeopardize the quality of the results and the experiment's credibility.

This is critical because statistical methods cannot correct flaws in experimental design or data collection, and even when they can, extensive work and firm assumptions are required (Kass, Eden, & Brown, 2014).

As a result, considerable effort must be expended to ensure that the cleanest data possible is recorded (Luck, 2014). To obtain reproducible and statistically significant experimental effects, low levels of noise must be achieved. Noise reduction is critical because it could be equivalent to doubling the number of trials or subjects in each experiment (Luck, 2014).

Noise can be reduced by increasing the number of trials, but this is not recommended because trials must be increased fourfold to reduce noise by half (Kappenman & Luck, 2010), which would significantly increase the experiment's budget and duration, rendering it unviable.

Another possibility is to reduce noise before it is detected by the device in use. In EEG research, for example, much of the noise comes from non-biological signals such as skin potentials and electrical noise sources in the environment that are accidentally picked up during recording.

Skin potentials could be reduced by keeping the recording environment consistently cool and dry to prevent skin abrasion beneath the electrode (Kappenman & Luck, 2010). Skin potentials could also be reduced by using a needle to puncture the skin at the recording site (Picton & Hillyard, 1972).

In addition to locating and eliminating noise sources, data-processing techniques such as filtering can be used to reduce noise (Luck, 2014). However, it is important not to rely too heavily on post-processing techniques because these techniques are only effective under certain conditions and almost always distort the data.

The best strategy is to eliminate all sources of noise before conducting an experiment to save one-third of the time required per participant. Pre-experiment noise reduction can reduce the impedance between the recording electrodes and the live skin tissue from 5k to an average of 2k, resulting in significantly better data quality.

In short, entrepreneurship scholars should take every precaution to obtain the cleanest data possible in order to improve data quality and significantly increase the likelihood of obtaining a statistically significant experimental effect (Kappenman & Luck, 2010). It will save both money and time.

Principle 3: for judgement and decision-making studies, consider a within-subject design

Before elaborating on why a within-subjects design is preferred in decision-making and judgement-related experiments, it is important to note that in a laboratory experiment, the researcher must decide whether to manipulate the independent variable between or within subjects (Wilson et al., 2010).

Within-subject design participants will be exposed to multiple treatments and their outcomes will be compared across treatment conditions (Mark & Reichardt, 2004). This design enables participants to examine and control the order in which they view each condition (Hsu et al., 2017). Participants serve as their own statistical control (Grégoire & Lambert, 2015). In a between designs design, participants are only exposed to one experimental treatment (between-subject design), while the control group is not (Hsu et al., 2017).

We recommend a within-subject design for decision-making and judgement issues for a variety of reasons. First, within-subject designs require fewer participants to achieve sufficient statistical power. Because the same individual responds to all treatments and serves as his own control, the sample size is a fraction of what would be required in a between-subject design (Hsu et al., 2017). Second, their internal validity is not dependent on random assignment (Simmons et al., 2016). Third, these designs are naturally compatible with the majority of theoretical mindsets (Charness, Gneezy, & Kuhn, 2012).

Furthermore, decision-making and judgement experiments are typically simpler to conduct because they require a less elaborate setting to involve participants in a meaningful situation (Wilson et al., 2010). Participants in this type of experiment behave more like passive observers, being asked to recognize, recall, classify, or evaluate stimuli presented by the experimenter (Wilson et al., 2010).

As a result, as long as treatments do not significantly alter participants' self-concepts, within-subject designs are well suited to decision-making and judgement experiments in entrepreneurship. Little direct impact on participants is required, and the stimulus must be sufficient to capture people's attention and elicit meaningful responses (Wilson et al., 2010).

For example, in the Forlani and Mullins (2000) experiment, each participant was presented with the profiles of four ventures and then asked to make a choice. In each venture profile, the two independent variables (variability and hazard) were manipulated at different levels. Because the participant responded to four different venture scenarios, the first decision could have influenced the subsequent one. Consequently, it was critical for Forlani and Mullins to randomly present the four venture scenarios to the participants to counterbalance potential carryover effects. These effects refer to the likelihood that a previous treatment may affect behaviour in a subsequent experimental treatment.

It should be noted that Forlani and Mullins could have used a between-subjects design as well. Such a design, however, would have quadrupled the sample size and significantly increased the cost of the experiment.

Principle 4: consider a between-subjects design for impact studies

A between-subjects design is recommended in impact-related experiments. People in impact experiments are active participants in a series of unfolding events and must react to those events as they occur (Wilson et al., 2010).

A between-subjects design involves exposing different groups of participants to varying levels of one or more target variables (Grégoire & Lambert, 2015). Participants are randomly assigned to either a treatment or a control condition, and the outcomes of these groups are compared (Mark & Reichardt, 2004).

There are compelling reasons why a between-subject design is appropriate for impact experiments in entrepreneurship. First, this design favour studies that have the potential to have a significant impact on people's self-perceptions (Wilson et al., 2010). People in impact experiments are active participants in a series of events that are unfolding and react to those events as they occur (Wilson et al., 2010). Second, because between-subject designs do not anchor participant responses after exposure to one treatment, they are not susceptible to carry-over effects (Wilson et al., 2010).

The assessment of the role of emotions in entrepreneurship, for example, corresponds to impact experiments because these are specifically designed to actively engage participants to the point of influencing their self-views.

This leads to two useful recommendations for entrepreneurship researchers. First and foremost, the method must be tailored to the hypothesis (Wilson et al., 2010). Second, the impact experiment is the only option if the interest is in what happens when a person's self-concept is engaged by a series of events that happen to that person.

Principle 5: aim for homogeneous sampling

A brain-driven entrepreneurship experimenter shall aim for homogeneous sampling for two reasons. First, neuroscience shows that variables such as age (Cabeza, 2002), gender (Schulte-Rüther, Markowitsch, Shah, Fink, & Piefke, 2008), education (Garibotto et al., 2008), and even language (Abutalebi, Cappa, & Perani, 2001) can influence psychological processes and neural activations (Laureiro-Martínez et al., 2014). Second, entrepreneur skills vary according to age, gender, and education (Arenius & Minniti, 2005; Blanchflower, 2004; Hayton & Cholakova, 2012). Failure to consider this suggestion may have an impact on the validity of the results.

Paying attention to participant homogeneity is critical because it can help reduce confounding variables such as age, gender, and education, among others. It should be noted that homogeneity influences the size of the sample required to conduct a laboratory experiment.

Finding homogeneous participants necessitates a calculated selection of participants based on a set of relevant traits that are useful to the study's hypothesis. Age and education, for example, are two relevant variables to consider in entrepreneurship research.

Is important to note that the sample size in homogeneous sampling is typically small, which is advantageous in entrepreneurship research because it reduces the cost of a study. In homogeneous sampling, a small sample size is justified for two reasons.

First, the deliberate selection of uniform participants reduces naturally the number of eligible subjects required in a study. Second, statistical analysis confirms that the optimal number of participants is 16 (Friston, 2012). Friston (2012) believes that if a researcher cannot demonstrate a significant effect with 16 subjects, the experiment should be abandoned. Desmond and Glover (2002), on the other hand, state that for a P-value threshold of 0.05, 12 subjects are required to achieve 80% power. Moreover, small sample sizes are also driven by logistical factors such as participant costs (Laureiro-Martinez, Venkatraman, Cappa, Zollo, & Brusoni, 2015).

Although the sample size in homogeneous sampling is generally small, entrepreneurship researchers should keep in mind that sample size varies marginally depending on the type of study. fMRI studies, for example, use samples of 15–20 people (Yarkoni & Braver, 2010).

Experiments aiming to explore individual differences employ samples of around 30 participants (Venkatraman, Huettel, Chuah, Payne, & Chee, 2011). Studies that compare the differences between two groups of people use samples of about 50 people.

Ortiz-Terán et al. (2014), for example, used a sample of 50 participants, 25 entrepreneurs and 25 non-entrepreneurs, to investigate the relationship between neurophysiologic and personality characteristics in entrepreneurial decision-making.

Finally, remember that between-subject designs typically require twice as many participants as within-subject designs (Maxwell, Delaney, & Kelley, 2017).

Principle 6: choose an appropriate manipulation

Choosing an appropriate manipulation is critical in a brain-driven entrepreneurship study, regardless of whether it is a between-subject or within-subject-based study. Two of the three manipulation types commonly used in entrepreneurship research could be adapted to a brain-driven approach. These are: information manipulations, treatment manipulations, and priming manipulations (Grégoire & Lambert, 2015).

Information manipulations consist in the systematic variation of information embedded in stories, scenarios, cases, profiles, descriptions, audio or video recordings in order to explain the reactions of participants (Grégoire & Lambert, 2015). Hsu et al. (2017) refer to this manipulation as passive role playing because it requires little participation from the participants. These manipulations are also known as vignettes or conjoint experiments (Hsu et al., 2017).

This type of manipulation is recommended for judgement studies because it usually requires participants to read a text or observe a phenomenon before passing judgements or making evaluations. The good news is that this manipulation is compatible with the brain-driven approach advocated in this book. It can be tested in a lab, and the data collected and processed using appropriate neuroscience technology.

On the other hand, treatment manipulations look into how different interventions affect participant's behaviour. Treatment manipulations in entrepreneurship frequently concern the effects of pedagogical methods (Grégoire & Lambert, 2015). Depending on the degree of realism, these manipulations may be classified as 'active participation' because they imply high involvement in a real-world context or 'passive participation' because they imply low involvement in a real-world context. The study of Souitaris et al. (2007) depicts a typical example of the use of this manipulation. Soutari's team recruited students to participate in an entrepreneurship training programme, then assessed the programme's impact on participants' entrepreneurial intentions. This experiment's participants were very involved because they actively participated in the experiment and responded to the manipulation (Hsu et al., 2017). Nonetheless, using this manipulation in the context of a brain-based entrepreneurship research approach is challenging for two reasons. First, the internal validity is low because experimenting in a real-world or near-real-world setting does not provide the same level of control as a laboratory setting. A lack of control may result in the emergence of extraneous variables that may affect the results of the experiment.

Second, except for EEG, none of the existing neuroscience techniques can handle the mobility requirements of treatment manipulations. Even simultaneous EEG recordings of several participants in a close-to-real-world setting would be difficult.

Lastly, priming manipulations use instructions, research material, and other aspects of an experiment's context to subconsciously prime or induce a specific state of mind (Grégoire & Lambert, 2015). Depending on the level of participant involvement, priming manipulations can be 'active role playing', which means high involvement in a simulated scenario, or 'passive role playing', which means low involvement in a hypothetical setting (Hsu et al., 2017).

Grichnik, Smeja, and Welpe (2010), for example, used movie clips to prime the positive and negative emotions embedded in a bogus visual acuity test before evaluating participants' entrepreneurial orientation. Because priming manipulations can influence participant's self-views (Bengtsson, Dolan, & Passingham, 2010), they could be used in both impact and judgement studies. Priming manipulations, like information manipulations, could be used in the context of a brain-driven research approach because they can be carried out in a laboratory and the data analysed using appropriate neuroscience technology.

Overall, when choosing a proper manipulation, a brain-driven entrepreneurship scholar must consider two critical factors: the manipulation can be implemented in a laboratory setting, and it may allow the use of a fitting neurotechnology.

Principle 7: aim for simplicity when searching or creating an experimental task

A key aspect of an experiment, aside from manipulation, is developing a comprehensive experimental task that is effective in capturing the independent variable while influencing no other factors (Wilson et al., 2010), that is the ability to best isolate the brain processes under investigation.

In general, when searching for or creating an experimental task, a brain-driven entrepreneurship experimenter should strive for simplicity. An experimental task is a simple, clear, and repeatable procedure that resembles a simulated scenario in which a decision is made several times (Laureiro-Martinez et al., 2015).

Because the type of manipulation is related to the level of elaboration of a task, the development of experimental tasks in information manipulations is simpler. Information manipulations only involve the display of text and images. As a result, a detailed set of instructions is sufficient to complete the task. Priming manipulations, nevertheless, necessitate a higher level of elaboration because they are aimed to examine specific cognitive processes without the participants' awareness (Bargh & Chartrand, 2000).

Tully and Boudewyn (2018) state that regardless of the type of manipulation, a well-designed experimental task should take three factors into account. First, consider the task's core elements, such as the stimulus, condition and trial numbers, and response format. Second, issues concerning experiment implementation, such as experimental modality, participant burden, and analysis plan; and third, the availability of both monetary and intangible resources.

Furthermore, the task should be repeatable and capable of holding participants' attention (Wilson et al., 2010). Simply put, the experimenter's challenge is to create tasks that participants can understand in the same way that the experimenter does (Webster & Sell, 2014).

Finally, brain-driven entrepreneurship researchers could also borrow and adapt existing experimental tasks from psychology and neuroscience, even combining tasks if it serves the research purpose best (Venkatraman, Rosati, Taren, & Huettel, 2009). The Stroop task, for example, can be used to assess cognitive functions such as attention (Lamers, Roelofs, & Rabeling-Keus, 2010) whereas the four-armed bandit task (Daw, O'Doherty, Dayan, Seymour, & Dolan, 2006) and the Kolling, Wittmann, and Rushworth (2014) task could both be employed to evaluate entrepreneurial decision-making issues.

Principle 8: fulfil the ethical requirements of your home institution

Entrepreneurship researchers must always verify their home institution's ethical guidelines (Levitin, 2002), as well as be ready to deal with ethical issues that arise when using neuroscience techniques.

Experimenting typically entails collecting self-reported behavioural or physiological data from human subjects in accordance with the ethical principles of human dignity, beneficence, and justice (Weijer et al., 2016).

Human subjects research is reviewed and approved by committees at most universities to ensure that subjects are treated ethically, and that fair and humane procedures are followed (Levitin, 2002). However, compliance with ethical standards varies by university (Levitin, 2002). Some universities provide automatic ethical approval for EEG or transcranial direct current stimulation (TDCS) studies, whereas others do not. Ethical approval is always required for fMRI studies.

Aside from traditional ethical standards, entrepreneurship scholars employing a brain-driven research approach require a comprehensive protocol for dealing with incidental findings, which refers to all physical abnormalities discovered in brain scans following data collection (Laureiro-Martinez et al., 2015).

This is not a minor concern; evidence suggests that accidental discoveries in neuroscience occur (Katzman, Dagher, & Patronas, 1999), and many fMRI studies are conducted by non-physicists, allowing for unanticipated outcomes that may go undetected, leaving subjects without appropriate referral (Illes, Desmond, Huang, Raffin, & Atlas, 2002). Aside from fMRI, other neurotechnologies such as magnetoencephalography (MEG) and electroencephalography (EEG) can detect anomalies (Nelson, 2008).

Thus, detecting, interpreting, and managing incidental findings is critical to participants' well-being as well as the experiment's integrity (Illes et al., 2002).

Since there is no guidance for addressing this issue in the camp of entrepreneurship, we provide four recommendations (Illes et al., 2006) to deal properly with incidental findings. First, determine the possibility of incidental findings at the start of the study rather than later. Second, if there is a chance of a significant incidental finding create a procedure for discovering and reporting such findings. Third, establish the reporting threshold for incidental findings and fourth, if monitoring and reporting incidental findings is impractical or overly burdensome the ethical committee should be approached.

As the adoption of protocols to deal with incidental findings is critical in the context of a brain-driven entrepreneurship era, it is expected that it will happen soon.

Principle 9: undertake a post-experimental follow-up

It is critical to conduct post-experimental follow-up. Although most of the experiment's success is determined by the quality of the design and data, the challenge does not end there.

A cautious experimenter should conduct a thorough follow-up to ensure the experiment's validity. This can be accomplished through four measures: ensuring that participants are in good health; ensuring they comprehend the experimental procedure, hypothesis, and their own performance; looking for signs of scepticism and utilizing participants' unique skills as valuable consultants for the study; because only the participants can determine whether or not the instructions were clear, whether or not the independent variable had the desired effect on them, and so forth (Wilson et al., 2010).

Similarly, the participants must be persuaded not to discuss the experiment with others until it is completed. Failure to do so may result in a few uninformed participants undermining the entire study (Wilson et al., 2010). Furthermore, post-experimental follow-up is required in a brain-driven entrepreneurship era because most neuroscience techniques are unfamiliar and, to some extent, frightening to participants.

The application of the nine experimentation principles is critical because it ensures an accurate exploration of a set of themes that we believe would be best approached using a brain-driven approach. Each of these themes is expanded on in the following section.

Part III
Fitting themes and empirical evidence

5 Fitting themes

A brain-driven approach to entrepreneurship can and should be used to address questions that cannot be easily assessed with conventional methods. For instance, what goes through the brain of an entrepreneur who sees an opportunity, seizes it, or employs bricolage? How quickly do entrepreneurs sight opportunities? (Hoskisson, Covin, Volberda, & Johnson, 2011), How can entrepreneurs' cognitive performance be improved? How can students' entrepreneurship education be improved?

These are the kind of questions that match the entrepreneurs brain era. This section provides a first look at some, but not all, of the entrepreneurship hot topics that could be investigated using a brain-driven perspective. These refer to entrepreneurial decision making, emotions, self-efficacy, working memory, perception, attention, well-being and mental health.

5.1 Decision-making

Decision-making is the only topic that has already begun to be assessed using a brain-driven approach. The use of EEG and fMRI has revealed that entrepreneurs make faster and more efficient decisions than non-entrepreneurs (Laureiro-Martínez et al., 2014; Ortiz-Terán et al., 2014).

The term 'decision' signifies that the period of deliberation has come to an end and that action has begun (Buchanan & Connell, 2006). Decision-making is a popular (Clarke & Cornelissen, 2014; Maine, Soh, & Dos Santos, 2015), well-established (Baron & Ward, 2004; Shepherd, Williams, & Patzelt, 2015), and timely topic for entrepreneurship researchers (Shane, 2003; Shane & Venkataraman, 2000).

A brain-driven approach has the capabilities to examine decision-making issues (Schade, 2005); thus, it should be utilized to examine the four stages of entrepreneurial decision-making: recognition of the current state, evaluation of alternatives, action selection, and outcome re-evaluation (Doya, 2008).

DOI: 10.4324/9781003057109-8

Entrepreneurial decision-making could also be evaluated during opportunity evaluation, entry, exploitation, and exit (Shepherd et al., 2015), taking into account its rational, emotional, or intuitive variants (De Winnaar & Scholtz, 2019).

It is well known that entrepreneurs face a variety of differences that influence the evaluation of a business opportunity, the start-up of a new venture, the exploitation of a venture, and the exit of a venture (Shepherd et al., 2015). At the end of the day, the effectiveness of the resulting decisions determines success or failure.

For example, decision-making differences related to emotional reaction (Welpe, Spörrle, Grichnik, Michl, & Audretsch, 2012), beliefs and desires (Shepherd et al., 2015), aspirations and attitudes (Birley & Westhead, 1994), abilities (Elfenbein, Hamilton, & Zenger, 2010), self-perception (Fauchart & Gruber, 2011), and even perception of morality (McVea, 2009) could be addressed more effectively with neurotechnologies than with traditional approaches.

Quality and speed are also important issues in decision-making (Symmonds et al., 2013). For instance, a brain-driven approach could be used to investigate what happens in the entrepreneur's brain when they make decisions (Foo, Murnieks, & Chan, 2014), as well as to examine the inverse relationship between decision-making speed and performance (i.e., the speed-accuracy trade-off) (Bogacz, Wagenmakers, Forstmann, & Nieuwenhuis, 2010). In this way, neurotechnologies may aid in improving decision-making efficiency, or the ability to generate quick responses while maintaining adequate performance.

5.2 Emotions and emotion regulation

Emotions, particularly emotion regulation, are the second theme that could benefit from a brain-driven approach. Because the entrepreneurial journey is frequently described as an emotional roller coaster (De Cock, Denoo, & Clarysse, 2020), entrepreneurs are more frequently and intensely exposed to emotional cues than ordinary people (Grégoire & Lambert, 2015).

For example, emotions such as passion, happiness, joy, anxiety, fear, hope, and anger (Foo, 2011; Hayton & Cholakova, 2012; Mitteness, Sudek, & Cardon, 2012; Welpe et al., 2012) hold the power to influence entrepreneur's decision-making throughout the venture creation process (Cacciotti & Hayton, 2015; Cardon, Foo, Shepherd, & Wiklund, 2012; De Winnaar & Scholtz, 2019; Lerner, Li, Valdesolo, & Kassam, 2015; Nieto, Fernández-Abascal, & Miguel-Tobal, 2009; Rolls, 2014; Shepherd & Patzelt, 2018; Shepherd et al., 2015; Treffers, Welpe, Spörrle, & Picot, 2017).

Emotions are therefore a critical component in entrepreneurship (Arpi-ainen, Täks, Tynjälä, & Lackéus, 2013; Jones & Underwood, 2017; Lack-éus, 2014) and a powerful driver of entrepreneurial behaviour (Cardon, Wincent, Singh, & Drnovsek, 2009; Fodor & Pintea, 2017).

Neurotechnologies, for example, could be used to assess the brain pro-cesses that underpin entrepreneurs' higher levels of negative (Brundin & Gustafsson, 2013) and positive emotions (Tata, Martinez, Garcia, Oesch, & Brusoni, 2017) such as passion, envy, anger, and fear of failure (Biniari, 2012; Cacciotti & Hayton, 2015; Cardon et al., 2009; Foo, 2011).

Neurotechnologies may also be useful in carrying out more in-depth analyses of the relationship between emotions and entrepreneurial decision-making (Lerner et al., 2015; Zhu, 2015), high risk (Baron, 2008), learning (Pless, Maak, & Stahl, 2011), and successful venture creation.

Neurotechnologies can aid in better understanding the relationship between so-called emotional competencies (Fernández-Pérez, Montes-Merino, Rodríguez-Ariza, & Galicia, 2019) and anticipated emotions (Zampetakis, Lerakis, Kafetsios, & Moustakis, 2015) in entrepreneurship education, particularly action-based pedagogies (Lackéus, 2014).

Furthermore, neurotechnologies could be used to boost positive emo-tional responses in order to accelerate entrepreneurial success; we believe that research on this topic should be prioritized.

All of this suggests that a brain-driven perspective can help in further understanding one of the more enigmatic subjects in the field of entrepre-neurship: entrepreneurs' emotions.

5.3 Well-being and mental health

Entrepreneurs' well-being and mental health are promising topics (Wiklund et al., 2020) that can and should be addressed from a brain-driven per-spective. Entrepreneurial well-being is characterized as 'the experience of satisfaction, positive affect, infrequent negative affect, and psychological functioning in relation to developing, starting, growing, and running an entrepreneurial venture' (Wiklund, Nikolaev, Shir, Foo, & Bradley, 2019). It is worth noting that the components of well-being are linked to cognitive and affective processes that come from the entrepreneur's brain.

Among the issues encompassed by the theme of entrepreneurial well-being and mental health, one deserves special attention: the relationship between the attention deficit hyperactivity disorder (ADHD) and entrepre-neurial success.

Wiklund, Patzelt, and Dimov (2016) reveal that ADHD symptoms such as poor concentration, hyperactivity, and a lack of self-regulation appear to impair performance in general, but there is evidence that, in the case of entrepreneurs diagnosed with ADHD, these traits contribute to the achievement of venture success. For example, entrepreneurs with ADHD appear to exhibit high levels of passion, hyperfocus, physical restlessness, persistence, and intuitive decision-making in uncertain situations, which puts them on the fast track to business success (Wiklund et al., 2016).

Since ADHD symptoms originate in the entrepreneur's brain, a brain-driven approach would be most effective in determining the role of ADHD in entrepreneurial success and identifying novel treatments to upregulate or downregulate the manifestation of their traits, depending on the circumstances.

In addition to studying ADHD, it is crucial to investigate the interaction of stressors resulting from overwork, as the brain-driven approach advocated in this book may lead to the discovery of new mechanisms to regulate their manifestation.

5.4 Perception

The fourth priority topic that should be researched using brain-driven lenses is perception. The reason is straightforward: for a business opportunity to be detected, it must first be detected by the entrepreneur's brain, which means it must be consciously perceived. Low perception skills imply that there is no chance of identifying any business opportunity at all. To put it simply, perception is the organization, identification, and interpretation of sensory information in order to represent and comprehend the presented information or environment (Schacter, Gilbert, Nock, & Wegner, 2020).

The Wright brothers' rise to prominence as aviation pioneers is a good example of the importance of perception in high-value entrepreneurship.

When they looked up at the sky, they 'perceived' something that no one else did. While most people saw only a beautiful blue sky, they saw the possibility of flying. Consider what might have happened if the Wright Brothers had not been so foresighted.

Despite the importance of perception skills for entrepreneurial success, little scholarly attention is paid to the underpinnings of perception during opportunity recognition and exploitation, particularly in terms of sensory stimulation and selection, organization, and interpretation. Current research rather focuses on the origins of business ideas and the identification of opportunities, but from the wrong angle. The key is to look at how a successful entrepreneur's brain developed such capacity over time rather than what he says about how he discovered a business opportunity.

Perception is an excellent and appropriate research topic within the framework of the brain-driven approach. However, it should be noted that it is not enough to investigate how aspiring entrepreneurs' perception skills develop; it is also necessary to investigate how this capacity can be nurtured and improved over time. The framework presented in this book contains the seeds to meet this challenge.

5.5 Memory

Unlike attention and perception, memory has received little attention as a relevant skill for entrepreneurial success (Baron & Henry, 2010). Memory in essence, refers to cognitive systems that store information (Baddeley, 1997) so that it can be processed and used later.

Working memory is one type of memory, and we believe it is essential for high-quality entrepreneurship simply because working memory skills are closely related to reasoning, decision-making, and behaviour (Barkley, 2001).

Therefore, it can be stated that every entrepreneur who consistently makes rational and effective decisions has a brain with strong working memory capacities. If effective decision-making can lead to greater entrepreneurial success, then Elon Musk's brain may have solid memory abilities. In contrast, it can be inferred that an entrepreneur who continues to make poor decisions due to a deficient memory has little chance of achieving success.

Existing conventional research methods in entrepreneurship can at least examine the outward manifestations of cognitive processes, such as memory but they are unable to provide further assistance to aspiring entrepreneurs with poor memory skills. A brain-driven approach, such as the one introduced in these texts, can.

Future research should therefore focus on elucidating new mechanisms to specifically improve the working memory of aspiring entrepreneurs before and after business formation. Again, a brain-driven approach aided by cutting-edge neurotechnologies is well-suited to explore novel ways to foster and improve the working memory of entrepreneurs.

5.6 Attention

Attention, like perception and working memory, is a crucial executive function that, in this brain-driven era, merits additional study. Because attention can be defined in a variety of ways, let us clarify that in this case, attention is regarded as a mechanism for selecting information to be processed with priority (Chun, Golomb, & Turk-Browne, 2011). The reasoning is straightforward: the better an entrepreneur's attention skills, the more likely his brain will be able to focus on and capitalize on relevant information for the successful identification and exploitation of a business opportunity.

Consider whether the original Macintosh could have achieved the same level of success without the iconic mouse device. Imagine what the fate of the Apple computer could have been if Steve Jobs had not focused on the mouse, windows, and icons during his 1979 visit to Xerox PARC. Certainly, it was not Steve's merit; rather, it was his brain's attention skills that enabled him to spot, concentrate on, and profit from these items on a global scale. The issue of attention in entrepreneurship has received little attention thus far, even though the identification of any business opportunity requires an elevated level of attentional skills to focus on it once it has been detected by the entrepreneur's brain.

Future brain-driven research should therefore look into the role of attention throughout the entrepreneurial process, particularly during the stage of identifying business opportunities. The enhancement of selective attention, in particular, should be investigated because it deals with the ability to concentrate on one item while mentally dismissing all other irrelevant information. This is precisely the path taken by successful entrepreneurs; once they identify a business opportunity, they devote their entire attention to it until the end.

5.7 Volition

Volition, despite its significance, is one of the rare research topics in the field of entrepreneurship that could be examined most effectively from a brain-driven perspective. We understand volition as an instance of central control that coordinates mental processes and subsystems in order to maximise the execution of intentions (Zhu, 2004). Entrepreneurially speaking, volition is the process that determines the transition from intention to action (Broonen, 2010), it is commonly known as 'will'.

The difference between the intention to become an entrepreneur and the consistent behaviour required to do so is bridged by volitional skills. Imagine the determination of Japanese entrepreneur Ikutaru Kakehashi, who was forced to abandon his business due to tuberculosis, then returned to business so close to death and more ill than before, reopened his shop, and founded the Roland Corporation. As evidenced by the evidence, enormous motivation and intention are insufficient (Hikkerova, Ilouga, & Sahut, 2016); what could have been mobilized instead Kakehashi is a set of highly developed volitional abilities cultivated by his brain at some point in his life.

A brain-based approach should therefore investigate the foundations of volitional skills among students, potential entrepreneurs, and active entrepreneurs. As per Hikkerova et al. (2016), these volitional skills are self-motivation (pre-decision), self-regulation, self-determination, resistance to uncertainty (pre-action), proactivity, concentration, and action orientation (action). We also believe that a brain-driven perspective should be used to discover ways to improve future entrepreneurs' volitional skills.

It should be noted that this is the first group of priority topics that may benefit from brain-based research. Chapter 13 provides an expanded list of suitable themes. With this in mind, the following section describes how a brain-driven approach was used to investigate an existing research gap in the field.

6 The function of emotions on entrepreneurial decision-making

This section provides an empirical illustration of the application of a brain-driven methodology to a current research gap in the field. Using electroencephalography and the event-related potentials technique, the experiment was conducted for the first time to investigate the relationship between emotional word stimuli and decision-making. The following section describes the experiment's major components, including participants, experimental task, procedure, trial duration, and initial findings.

6.1 Participants

The study included 32 international students from the University of Kobe. Due to equipment failure or data collection issues, 14 data sets were excluded. The remaining 18 participants (11 Female, 7 Male; age range = 18–25 years) were paid an honorarium ($10/hour) plus an additional payment if their final score exceeded the baseline of allocated game coins (18,000).

6.2 One armed-bandit task

Stimuli included a one-armed bandit task, classical decision-making stimuli (Daw et al., 2006), and the subliminal display of 16 subliminal emotional primers. Using the English Word Database of Emotional Terms (EMOTE) (Grühn, 2016) as a guide and event-related potential (ERP) evidence for differential processing of visually presented pleasant and unpleasant words (Bernat, Bunce, & Shevrin, 2001), we included the following primers: marvellous, superb, pleasure, beautiful, joyful, glorious, lovely, and wonderful (pleasant) and tragic, horrible, agony, painful, terrible, awful, humiliate (unpleasant).

Participants were shown an image of a slot machine and asked to bet or withdraw money with the primary goal of making the most profit (returns

DOI: 10.4324/9781003057109-9

Table 1 Slot machine returns

	Low	Middle	High
Average	0.46	3.09	5.99
SD	35.04	69.83	139.97
Max.	150.00	200.00	300.00
Min.	−50.00	−99.99	−199.95

maximization). Three distinct slot machine images were shown at random, one at a time, and were linked to any of the following conditions: 1) Low risk and low return: participants could win 50 game coins but lose the same amount. 2) High risk and high reward: participants may receive 200 game coins but may also lose the same number of coins. 3) Middle risk and middle reward: participants may receive 100 game coins but may also lose 100 game coins (see Table 1). Participants began the task with 18,000 game coins, and the betting amount was set to 100 game coins in each trial. The task was completed untimed to enable encoding of stimulus duration, memorization of stimulus duration, and decision-making (Klapproth, 2008).

6.3 Procedure

The experiment was carried out in an electrically shielded room. Participants were seated approximately 55 cm from a monitor that presented both the subliminal emotional primer in word format and a one-armed bandit task from a computer running Inquisit 5 (Computer software) retrieved from www.millisecond.com. Participants were engaged in the task while EEG data were recorded concurrently on a separate computer through Acknowledge 4.0 (Biopac Systems Inc., Goleta, CA).

Participants were instructed to use their right hand to press a mouse key to choose between betting and withdrawing from a randomly displayed slot machine (low, middle, or high risk). To bet, left-click, and to withdraw, right-click. Following three practice trials, participants made untimed, repeated choices from a single EEG-run of 180 trials. Participants were briefed after the conclusion of the experiment.

6.4 Trial timing

Each trial began with a fixation cross (+) for 800 ms, preceded by 70 ms of word priming triggers and an image of one of three slot machines (low, middle, and high risk) presented once at a time. The decision was not time

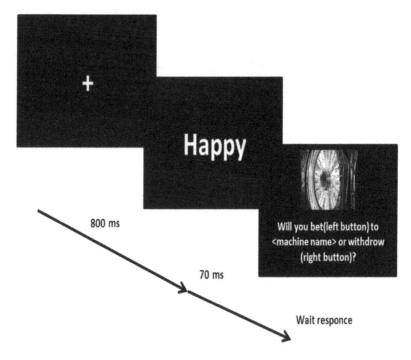

Figure 4 Trial timing diagram for the decision-making task

Source: own elaboration

constrained. The trial timing diagram for the decision-making task is shown in Figure 4.

6.5　Initial findings

This is the first experiment that uses a brain-based approach to look at how emotion-word cues affect entrepreneurial decision-making.

Three findings stand out. First, positive words cause a faster reaction time. Simply put, when participants are exposed to pleasant word stimuli, they tend to make quicker decisions.

Second: in high-risk situations, the reaction time is lengthened. In other words, participants tend to delay making decisions in high-risk situations.

Third, the experiment reveals the presence of two ERP components, the N100 and N400, which emerge as novel markers for assessing how an entrepreneur's brain processes emotions and decision making in greater depth. According to the evidence, the high-risk condition elicited a greater N100 response from participants than the middle-risk condition. In the same way, a high-risk condition, and the component N400 were found to have a positive relationship among the participants. The fact that the component N100 is reliant on stimulus unpredictability and the component N400 is associated with visual word stimuli suggests that these components have the potential to recognise and assess the role of emotions in entrepreneurial behaviour.

Electroencephalography and event-related potentials are not the only techniques capable of studying the entrepreneur's brain. Following is a discussion of the neurotechnologies that can be used to map entrepreneurs' brains, assess their brain activity, and enhance their conative, affective, and cognitive performance.

Part IV
The techniques of the future

7 Techniques for recording and assessing brain activity

A brain-driven approach also permits the real-time recording and evaluation of the brain activity of entrepreneurs. This section discusses two techniques for assessing entrepreneur brain activity: electroencephalography (EEG) and event-related potentials (ERPs).

7.1 EEG

EEG has been scarcely used in entrepreneurship research with two purposes, explore and compare decision-making speed and entrepreneurial behaviour during opportunity discovery on entrepreneurs and non-entrepreneurs (Ortiz-Terán et al., 2014; Zaro, da Cruz Fagundes, Rocha, & Nunes, 2016).

EEG recordings hold the capacity to measure brain activity in human subjects (Woodman, 2010). EEG is a safe technique (Bear, Connors, & Paradiso, 2007) that records electrical signals from the brain via a series of sensors attached on the scalp (Eysenck & Keane, 2000).

EEG is also capable to assess specific states of consciousness with an excellent temporal resolution (Carter & Shieh, 2015). However, one of its drawbacks is that it has a low spatial resolution (Bear et al., 2007). It is difficult to pinpoint where the electrical activity is coming from in the brain. EEG and tDCS are the most economical technologies when compared to MEG and fMRI (Bear et al., 2007).

7.2 ERPs

EEG recordings alone are not enough to explore entrepreneurs' cognitive processes. But when EEG works in tandem with a technique known as 'event-related potentials' (ERPs), it enables researchers to examine how brain activity is modulated in response to a specific task (Gazzaniga, Ivry, & Mangun, 2014).

DOI: 10.4324/9781003057109-11

The following is the logic of ERPs: EEG traces are averaged together from a series of trials by aligning them relative to an external event, such as the onset of a stimulus or response (Gazzaniga et al., 2014).

This alignment removes variations in the electrical activity of the brain that are unrelated to the events of interest. The evoked response, also known as the event-related potential (ERP), is a small signal encapsulated in the ongoing EEG that is triggered by the stimulus (Gazzaniga et al., 2014). By averaging the traces, it is possible to extract this signal which reflects the neural activity related to the sensory, motor, or cognitive event that triggered it (Gazzaniga et al., 2014)

ERPs holds gold value for entrepreneurship because it permits a detailed examination of a variety of cognitive functions (Bunge & Kahn, 2009). The fact that ERP yields a measure between stimulus and response, facilitates a much better understanding of the effects of experimental manipulations than behavioural responses (Bear et al., 2007). Put it simply, ERPs provide a continuous measure of the processes that take place between stimulus and response, making it possible to estimate which stage or stages of processing are affected by a particular experimental manipulation (Luck, 2014); with the unique advantage of affording online measures of the processing of stimuli, even in the absence of behavioural response (Luck, 2014). This advantage is not available through any traditional entrepreneurship research technique. However, it is prudent to choose research questions with the understanding that ERP recordings are small and require a large number of trials to accurately measure brain responses to specific stimuli (Luck, 2014).

Other ways, the strengths of ERPs have been put in action to investigate cognitive processes such as selective attention, decision processes, and language (Brandeis & Lehmann, 1986). Now is an excellent time to promote the use of ERPs in entrepreneurship, particularly in the study of critical cognitive processes for entrepreneurs such as attention and decision-making.

The reason for using ERPs in the case of attentional processes is obvious; attention is one of the earliest cognitive processes that occurs between an entrepreneur and the outside world, where business opportunities exist. Using ERPs, a thorough examination of entrepreneurs' attentional processes from discovery to exploitation could be possible. Because of their low spatial resolution, ERPs are better suited to questions about the speed of neural activity rather than the location of such activity.

While ERPs' strength lies in their ability to observe brain activity in real time, at the millisecond level (thousandths of a second), they are unable to determine where the electrical activity is coming from in the brain. Brain mapping technologies, as described in the following section, are the most effective methods for determining functional localization issues.

8 Techniques for mapping brain activity

A brain-driven approach facilitates the implementation of localisation studies. This section goes over two methods for mapping entrepreneur brain activity: functional magnetic resonance imaging (fMRI) and magneto-encephalography (MEG). Due to their capacity to assess the timing and location of brain activation during a variety of cognitive tasks, these techniques are able to contribute to a greater understanding of human cognition (Eysenck, 2006; Pushkarskaya, Smithson, Liu, & Joseph, 2010). These technologies are also known as brain imaging techniques.

8.1 FMRI

The application of fMRI should be expanded in the entrepreneurship brain era. This technology has been scarcely confined to explore decision-making (Laureiro-Martínez et al., 2014; Shane et al., 2020). The primary goal of fMRI is to pinpoint local variations in the BOLD signal in the brain and their correlation in a given task (Charron et al., 2008).

It employs a magnetic resonance imaging (MRI) machine to track blood-flow changes in the brain, which are thought to be correlated with local changes in neuronal activity (Eysenck & Keane, 2000; Gazzaniga et al., 2014).

In a typical fMRI experiment, a subject is exposed to a strong magnetic field, and the device records differences in the magnetic field caused by a local increase in blood flow in the brain. The outcome of this exercise is a blood-oxygenation-level-dependent signal known also BOLD signal. The BOLD signal is said to be an accurate representation of brain activity.

This technique is extremely effective because it can capture physiological changes on a timescale of hundreds of milliseconds, making it excellent for mapping the regions involved in task performance (Fox & Raichle, 2007). As a result, fMRI is ideal for determining the 'where', that is, which parts of the brain are in charge of critical functions.

DOI: 10.4324/9781003057109-12

In general fMRI can help to best understand cognition in a variety of way (Mather, Cacioppo, & Kanwisher, 2013). For starters, fMRI can provide answers to questions about which functions can be assigned to specific brain regions. Second, fMRI data can be used to identify specific mental processes, looking deeper into which processes are active during multiple tasks. Third, fMRI can provide answers to questions about how information is represented in each part of the brain. Fourth, fMRI can also determine whether two tasks use the same or different processing mechanisms.

Therefore, for the benefit of a brain-driven era to entrepreneurship, fMRI can scrutinize with precision a wide range of relevant cognitive functions (Cabeza & Nyberg, 2000). For example, the abilities of fMRI to investigate short-term working memory (D'Esposito, Postle, & Rypma, 2000), encoding and retrieval into long-term memory (Mcintosh, 1998), and attention (LaBar, Gitelman, Parrish, & Mesulam, 1999) should be applied to entrepreneurship.

Furthermore, fMRI should be used to advance our understanding of important entrepreneurship issues such as the role of emotions (Morris, Pryor, & Schindehutte, 2012; Norris, Coan, & Johnstone, 2007), emotional processing (Rämä et al., 2001), and decision-making (Michl, Welpe, Spörrle, & Picot, 2009).

This is possibly the most difficult technique to master, but learning to use it is essential. fMRI will become a crucial neurotechnology in this new era of entrepreneurship.

8.2 MEG

There is nowadays no entrepreneurship study that has profited from MEG's advantages. The magnetic fields produced by electrical activity in the brain are evaluated using this technique (Bear et al., 2007; Eysenck & Keane, 2000).

MEG measures the magnetic fields produced by electrical brain activity using a superconducting quantum interference device (SQUID) (Eysenck, 2006). This assessment can only be performed in a magnetically shielded room with no external magnetic properties that could conflict with the MEG signal (Charron et al., 2008). This technique is a bit complicated because the brain's magnetic field is highly small in comparison to the Earth's magnetic field (Eysenck, 2006).

MEG, like EEG, has a high temporal resolution (Eysenck, 2006), making it an excellent tool for studying brain mechanisms (Bunge & Kahn, 2009). Unlike EEG, MEG has a higher spatial resolution (2–3 mm) (Bear et al., 2007).

MEG has five pluses. It is non-invasive and well-tolerated by humans, it can be used with a variety of experimental paradigms, MEG can record data from the entire brain at the same time and equally important this technique can yield insight into the combined location and timing of cortical activity with accuracy unrivalled by any other technique.

Because magnetic fields pass more easily through the skull and scalp, MEG has better source localization than EEG. Nevertheless, the inverse problem is an issue for MEG as it is still hard to fully identify the generating neural sources from a MEG recording (Ruff & Huettel, 2014).

This method is frequently used to investigate a wide range of cognitive functions, for instance, MEG has been used to gauge the lateralization-localization of language functions (Roberts, Ferrari, Perry, Rowley, & Berger, 2000), the localization of memory processes (Castillo et al., 2001), emotions (Parkes, Perry, & Goodin, 2016), and attention (Assadollahi & Pulvermüller, 2001).

Since a further understanding of these cognitive functions is of utmost interest to entrepreneurship, MEG could for instance be used to investigate the role of executive functions behind efficient decision-making on entrepreneurs. This is just one of many entrepreneurship topics that could benefit from MEG's potential.

Beyond mapping brain functions with fMRI and MEG, we believe that the ultimate goal of a brain-driven era in entrepreneurship is the enhancement of the entrepreneurial brain. In this light, the section that follows elaborates on two approaches that have the potential to improve the brain performance of the entrepreneur.

9 Approaches for entrepreneurial enhancement

One of the greatest benefits of employing a brain-driven approach is that it is equipped with the technologies and theoretical framework necessary to cultivate, measure, and enhance the business performance of entrepreneurs. This section discusses two brain-driven approaches that may help to improve entrepreneurial performance: brain training and brain stimulation.

9.1 Brain training

Brain training can produce behavioural, neuroanatomical, and functional changes (Rabipour & Raz, 2012) which could help to improve key abilities such as cognitive flexibility, episodic memory, resilience, positivity bias, and motor processing. The development of most of these skills is essential for entrepreneurial success.

In short, brain training entails the entrepreneurs' participation in a programme or activity that aims to improve a cognitive skill through repetition over a limited period of time, it is also known as cognitive training.

Cognitive training can be delivered in a variety of ways, including process-based interventions such as repetitive exercise-like training on specific tasks or a more strategic and individualized intervention based on memory formation strategies such as the loci method or mnemonic history (Walton et al., 2015). Brain training must be done over time (Walton et al., 2015).

There are three major brain training approaches to improving cognitive functions with the aid of a computer, these are brain training programmes, working memory training programmes, and video game training programmes (Boot & Kramer, 2014).

Brain training programmes can help improve the speed and accuracy of perceptual processes, executive function, episodic memory and visual spatial skills (Klimova, 2016), reasoning (Corbett et al., 2015), attention

DOI: 10.4324/9781003057109-13

(Katwala, 2016), and the brain's ability to learn and adapt (Zinke et al., 2014).

There are five proven brain training apps available: Elevate: a cognitive training tool that aims to improve analytical and communication skills (Elevate, 2022); Lumosity: a series of online games that aim to improve memory, speed, problem solving, attention, and flexibility (Lumosity, 2022); Fit Brains: an app that focuses on improving mental performance through games (FitBrains, 2022); Brain HQ, which offers a series of training exercises that can improve visual scene processing, working memory, and cognitive flexibility (BrainWorkshop, 2022) and Brain workshop which is an application designed to improve working memory and fluid intelligence (BrainWorkshop, 2022).

The working memory programmes are designed to improve working memory, which is a fundamental cognitive ability for entrepreneurs (Baron, 2013). It symbolizes a system that maintains multiple pieces of temporary information in the mind, information that is required for various ongoing tasks (Klimova, 2016). This kind of programmes could improve short-term memory (McAvinue et al., 2013) and working memory capacity (Hyer et al., 2016).

Lastly, video game training programmes could also be an effective tool for improving cognitive functions such as interference resolution and working memory (Anguera et al., 2013). There is, however, a surge in online cognitive exercise products, whose efficacy has not been proven (Kueider, Parisi, Gross, & Rebok, 2012). Commercial cognitive training programmes, such as CogMed, Jungle Memory, or Cognifit, do not provide a theoretical explanation of the training mechanism behind the claimed improvement (Melby-Lervåg & Hulme, 2013).

Although that some evidence shows that computer-based cognitive training has minor effects on improving cognitive functioning (Lampit, Hallock, & Valenzuela, 2014), the benefits of cognitive training deserve to be gauged among current and aspiring entrepreneurs because the improvement of their entrepreneurial performance requires the improvement of key cognitive functions such as memory (Ariely, 2008), attention, decision-making (Shepherd & Patzelt, 2015), visual processing (Cumming & Williams, 2012) in addition to peripheral vision (Chia, 2008).

The importance of visual processing is less obvious, but it is no less significant, given that 80% of the information used to make a decision comes from the sense of vision. Improved peripheral vision may also aid in entrepreneurial learning (Chia, 2008).

Hence, the design and validation of cognitive training protocols tailored to boost 'entrepreneurial enhancement' is part of the set of techniques that comes with a brain-driven research approach to entrepreneurship.

9.2 Brain stimulation

There are two non-invasive brain stimulation techniques that can help to enhance entrepreneurial performance, these are transcranial magnetic stimulation (TMS) and transcranial direct current stimulation (tDCS) (Dettmers et al., 2011). Both rely on the application of an electric or magnetic current to the skull, which modulates (stimulates or inhibits) neuronal and brain activity (Hernández-Gutiérrez & Carrillo-Mora, 2017). Brain stimulation is an effective technique because it allows for the establishment of a causal relationship between cognitive processes and the function of specific brain areas (Miniussi, Harris, & Ruzzoli, 2013). Since EMT and tDCS can influence neuronal activity (Wagner, Valero-Cabre, & Pascual-Leone, 2007), they can be used to model cognitive functions (Veniero, Strüber, Thut, & Herrmann, 2016). For instance, that TMS and tDCS can increase dorsolateral pre-frontal cortex activity, specifically working memory performance (Brunoni & Vanderhasselt, 2014).

Taking into account that memory comprehends 'cold' and 'hot' cognitive processes (Hofmann, Schmeichel, & Baddeley, 2012) it is reasonable to consider that brain stimulation could be used to strengthen positive emotions, such as achievement emotions (Pekrun, Goetz, Frenzel, Barchfeld, & Perry, 2011) between aspiring entrepreneurs and entrepreneurs.

For instance, these techniques could facilitate the strengthening of emotions linked to entrepreneurial activity, such as passion, to accelerate the successful implementation of a venture (Cacciotti & Hayton, 2015; Delgado García, De Quevedo Puente, & Blanco Mazagatos, 2015).

To date, tDCS research has determined the optimal location, type, and size of current to produce specific effects (Howard-Jones, 2014b) in a variety of cognitive processes ranging from attention, visual target detection, memory visual, affect, word recognition memory, risk taking (Heinrichs, 2012) to decision-making (Ouellet et al., 2015).

TMS, on the other hand, is used to investigate a wide range of cognitive functions, including attention, episodic memory (including short- and long-term memory), language, and visual perception (Rossi, Hallett, Rossini, Pascual-Leone, & Group, 2009).

EMT has been shown to improve learning and performance in virtual reality military training games. Participants who received 2 mA of ETM therapy improved twice as much in terms of learning and performance as those who received 1/20 of the therapy (Clark et al., 2012). Transcranial electrical stimulation (TSE) (electrode-based), which is a variation of TMS (coil-based), has also been shown to improve learning processes (Howard-Jones, 2014b).

Because there is encouraging evidence that these techniques hold the ability to influence cognitive processes (Wagner et al., 2007), their application in entrepreneurship should be tried. The further investigation of specific mechanisms underlying the behavioural and physiological effects induced by brain stimulation (Dayan, Censor, Buch, Sandrini, & Cohen, 2013), should not act as an obstacle to start the application of these techniques on entrepreneurs. The graph in Figure 5 illustrates the neurotechnologies' strengths in function of the research goal.

In the context of the two approaches to entrepreneurial enhancement outlined in this section, there are three neurotechnologies that could be utilized to enhance the performance of the entrepreneurial brain in order to accelerate venture success. The following section describes these neurotechnologies in detail, which include neurofeedback, transcranial magnetic stimulation, and transcranial direct current stimulation.

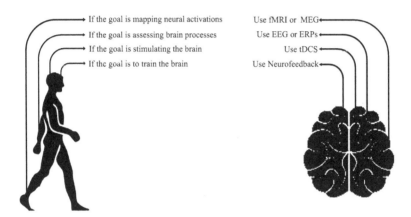

Figure 5 Criteria for the selection of appropriate neurotechnologies

Source: own elaboration

10 Techniques for entrepreneurial enhancement

This section focuses on three neurotechnologies that, when applied from a brain-driven perspective, may aid entrepreneurs in enhancing their venture creation and growth performance: neurofeedback, transcranial magnetic stimulation, and transcranial direct current stimulation.

10.1 Neurofeedback

Neurofeedback is another technique that belongs to this new brain era that aims to upgrade 'entrepreneurial performance'.

Unlike neurotools aimed at analysing and mapping brain activity such as electroencephalography (EEG), magnetoencephalography (MEG), and functional magnetic resonance imaging (fMRI), neurofeedback is a psychophysiological procedure in which a participant receives feedback based on neuronal activation for self-regulation purposes (Sitaram et al., 2016).

In other words, neurofeedback enables a person to monitor consciously their brain activity in real time and gradually influence it to achieve a specific goal (Howard-Jones, 2014b). Learning to control brain activity with neurofeedback is like cognitive training in that it is built through repetition (Sitaram et al., 2016).

In neurofeedback, brain activity is the independent variable while behaviour and thought are the dependent variables (Sitaram et al., 2016).

Evidence in the field of psychology tells that neurofeedback has been instrumental to improve creative performance (Howard-Jones, 2014a, 2014b), attention (Gruzelier, Foks, Steffert, Chen, & Ros, 2014), and cognitive skills learning (Yin et al., 2009).

Neuroscience evidence shows that neurofeedback can reduce fear memories and even change facial preferences on a subconscious level (Koizumi et al., 2016). This data opens a wide range of possibilities for the use of neurofeedback in entrepreneurship because it can help to elucidate new

DOI: 10.4324/9781003057109-14

neurofeedback-based training protocols to reduce the fear of failure, one of the biggest obstacles to entrepreneurship.

Moreover, neurofeedback can influence the plasticity of complex cognitive processes related to the formation of beliefs, cognition, emotions, including opportunity beliefs (Spezio & Adolphs, 2010). Because of its role in controlling action, habits, knowledge, and planning, neurofeedback can aid in the gradual modification of memory, a critical cognitive function for entrepreneurship (Baron, 2013; Logan, 2008).

On the other hand, preliminary pilot evidence on the use of neurofeedback among entrepreneurship students shows an increase in concentration metrics, improved emotional control, increased tolerance to workload and failure, improved self-efficacy, creativity, locus of control, and stress reduction (Rahmati, Rostami, Zali, Nowicki, & Zarei, 2014).

In short, this technique can induce specific behavioural changes (Sitaram et al., 2016), which could translate into the improvement of entrepreneur's cognitive skills and thereof, their entrepreneurial performance. For example, neurofeedback could be utilized to treat and mitigate one of the major barriers to entrepreneurship, the fear of failure (Cacciotti & Hayton, 2015).

Same as the typewriters could not compete with the world first personal computer, the Kenbak-1, neurofeedback is to play a critical role in the nurturing and improvement of entrepreneurial skills and in so doing disrupt the way entrepreneurship is taught.

10.2 Transcranial magnetic stimulation

TMS has not been used in entrepreneurship, despite its proven ability to stimulate nerve cells in the brain. It is an established research tool in cognitive neuroscience (Pascual-Leone, Grafman, & Hallett, 1994; Walsh & Cowey, 1998) because it can affect a specific region of the cortex by stimulating the brain. The behavioural outcomes of brain stimulation are used to learn more about the normal function of the disrupted tissue. This method is enticing because it facilitates a comparison between stimulated and non-stimulated conditions in the same person (Gazzaniga et al., 2014).

A usual TMS experiment means the placement of a coil (often of the shape of a 'eight') ear the participant's head (Eysenck, 2006). Then, a quick (less than 1 ms) but powerful magnetic pulse of current is passed through it. This generates a short-lived magnetic field that ordinarily inhibits processing in the involved brain area (Eysenck & Keane, 2000).

TMS embodies key features of utmost interest for entrepreneurship, for example, it enables non-invasive manipulation of neural processing with high spatial resolution and exceptional temporal resolution (Ruff & Huettel, 2014).

Second, TMS can be used quite flexibly in terms of temporal profiles and stimulation patterns, which can have different effects on neural processing and behaviour. Third, TMS can be used on healthy people (Rossi et al., 2009).

Furthermore, TMS enables the establishment of causal links between neural states and behaviour, whereas fMRI and MEG can only report covariations between brain activity and behaviour and cannot determine whether a given neural substrate is required for a specific behaviour (Walsh & Cowey, 2000).

TMS, like any neurotechnology, has drawbacks. Due to the drop-off of the magnetic field with increasing distance from the coil, it can only pin-point brain areas on the cortical surface (Ruff & Huettel, 2014). Moreover, the distracting and painful effect of noise and tactile sensatiohs produced by TMS may make comparing behavioural effects for different stimulation sites more difficult. Furthermore, TMS can make blind studies hard to conduct in which participants and/or experimenters are oblivious of specific stimulation conditions (Ruff & Huettel, 2014).

TMS is a part of the new entrepreneurial brain era because it has been used to assess cognitive functions since its inception (Walsh & Cowey, 2000). It has been used to assess perception (Amassian et al., 1993), attention (Ashbridge, Walsh, & Cowey, 1997), plasticity (Stefan, Kunesch, Cohen, Benecke, & Classen, 2000), decision-making (van't Wout, Kahn, Sanfey, & Aleman, 2005), and learning (Ashbridge et al., 1997). TMS's vast body of evidence in the modulation of cognitive functions will be useful in better understanding entrepreneurial phenomena.

TMS's strengths, for example, could be tailored to assess and compare the give-and-take of various prefrontal cortex regions linked to attentional (dorsolateral area), decision-making (ventrolateral area), and emotional responses (orbitofrontal area). The stimulation and further enhancement of these cognitive functions is critical for higher entrepreneurial performance

10.3 Transcranial direct current stimulation

Transcranial direct current stimulation (tDCS) is a non-invasive technique (Nitsche & Paulus, 2011) that can alter the behaviour of neurons or neural networks in a particular brain region based on the excitation or inhibition of neuronal activity (Lewis et al., 2016). Despite being an appealing tool that allows painless modulation of cortical activity and excitability through the intact skull, tDCS has not been used in entrepreneurship research.

tDCS holds the strength to evoke and modulate neuroplasticity in the cerebral cortex in order to produce long-lasting but reversible shifts in cortical excitability and behaviour (Nitsche, Kuo, Paulus, & Antal, 2015; Ouellet et al., 2015; Stagg & Nitsche, 2011).

From a technical standpoint, tDCS is straightforward. It consists of connecting two electrodes to the scalp and applying a steady electric potential difference, thus running a limited but constant electrical current flowing between them (Nitsche & Paulus, 2011; Ruff & Huettel, 2014).

There are four benefits that distinguish tDCS as a unique tool for the entrepreneurs' brain era. tDCs has the capacity to either up- or downregulate neural excitability with an excellent control condition. Furthermore, tDCS has no distracting side effects, is inexpensive, and is simple to use (Ruff & Huettel, 2014).

Nonetheless, because tDCS spatial resolution is much lower, it is difficult to conclude that neural processing changes only in a very focused cortical region (Ruff & Huettel, 2014). What is more, the behavioural effects of a single session are transient, lasting only a few tens of minutes at most (Stagg & Nitsche, 2011).

No limitation can overcome tDCS's unique strength for advancing entrepreneurship, which is its ability to modulate ongoing task-related neural activity in an untraceable manner (Ruff & Huettel, 2014).

The evidence suggests that tDCS can upgrade attention and memory (Bolognini, Fregni, Casati, Olgiati, & Vallar, 2010), as well as measure minor decision processes (Ruff & Huettel, 2014). and even altering decision-making behaviour (Boggio et al., 2010; Ouellet et al., 2015).

These are the characteristics that distinguish tDCS as a distinct brain-driven tool for enhancing current challenges in entrepreneurial cognition

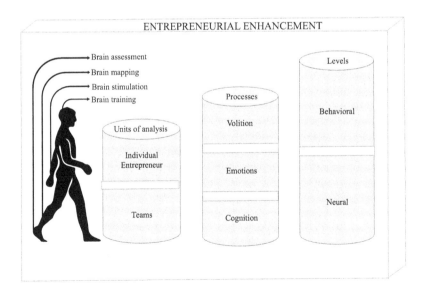

Figure 6 Drivers, processes, and levels of entrepreneurial enhancement.

Source: own elaboration

(Kincses, Antal, Nitsche, Bártfai, & Paulus, 2004), decision-making (Pripfl, Neumann, Köhler, & Lamm, 2013), and risk taking research (Minati, Campanha, Critchley, & Boggio, 2012). We believe that tDCS can help to best address these challenges. Figure 6 highlights the primary drivers, processes, and levels of entrepreneurial enhancement.

Up until now, one could rationalize the immense impact potential of these neurotechnologies. The following section discusses five ways in which a brain-driven era may disrupt the research, teaching, promotion, learning, and philosophy of entrepreneurship.

Part V

Foreseen disruptions and key implications

11 Foreseen disruptions

One essential distinction must be made before proceeding. In the traditional process-driven perspective of the management era of entrepreneurship, success is determined by the entrepreneur's capacity to navigate the business creation process (Shane & Venkataraman, 2000). Nonetheless in the context of a brain-driven approach, it is the entrepreneurs' brain which is behind failure or venture success. Keeping this in mind, this section examines the disruptive forces of the brain era in five fundamental areas of entrepreneurship: research, teaching, policymaking, learning, and philosophy.

11.1 Disrupt the way entrepreneurship is researched

Neuroscience is to refine the way entrepreneurship is studied. To date, entrepreneurship research has been majorly driven by methods derived from social sciences: quantitative, qualitative, and mixed methods, with the primary orientation on evaluating the past, that is, how a particular phenomenon did happen?

Yet, neuroscience's added value to entrepreneurship surpasses the exploration of the past and points to the analysis of the present (what is happening right now?) and the construction of a predictable future (How can this be improved?) The advent of these potentialities which have been hard to materialize by earlier stages in the history of entrepreneurship, is referred to as 'brain management' by Japanese neuroscientists.

In this direction, it is expected that the investigation of entrepreneurship is to transit towards a naturalistic approach grounded on the strengths of experimental design. This shift implies for instance that medicine-specific methodologies, like clinical-type trials will become the norm in entrepreneurship research.

A clinical trial, also known as experimental design, is one in which participants, are randomly assigned to one or more interventions (or a placebo

DOI: 10.4324/9781003057109-16

or no intervention) in order to assess the effects of such interventions (Neugebauer, Rothmund, & Lorenz, 1989; Thiese, 2014).

In general, clinical trials are applied to evaluate interventions ranging from the use of drugs to the use of medical devices for physiotherapy, acupuncture, and training (Röhrig, du Prel, Wachtlin, & Blettner, 2009). Clinical trials embrace the strength to best measure the efficiency of neuroscience-based interventions aimed to stimulate, or train entrepreneurial skills.

Clinical trials are therefore to be the ideal kind of design for the study of entrepreneurship (Shane, 2003) because this type of experimental approach could help to alleviate the discipline's major problem of internal validity (Krueger & Welpe, 2014). Needles to mention that the brain wave is to reposition the role of entrepreneurship researchers as entrepreneurship scientists.

11.2 Disrupt the way entrepreneurship is taught

Academics and political leaders agree that educational programmes that aim to produce entrepreneurs must cater to the social and economic requirements of all parties involved, including students, families, organizations, and nations (Fayolle, 2013).

Despite this, the efforts that are made to train entrepreneurs are not sufficient. First, because a major focus is placed on short-term subjective impact measures (Nabi, Liñán, Fayolle, Krueger, & Walmsley, 2016) based on attitudinal parameters and entrepreneurial intentions, rather than on long-term educational initiatives of greater impact linked, for example, to the creation of companies and entrepreneurial performance (Henry, Hill, & Leitch, 2005; Pittaway & Cope, 2007). Second, due to the lack of robust evidence on the link between the pedagogical efforts applied in the formation of entrepreneurs and the results achieved.

These weaknesses (Nabi et al., 2016) are reflected in the marginal effects achieved by existing educational efforts to train entrepreneurs through the development of their entrepreneurial intentions (Bae, Qian, Miao, & Fiet, 2014; Martin, McNally, & Kay, 2013). This indicates that entrepreneurship education thus far has been unable to demonstrate convincing results.

Evidence on the relationship between neuroscience, teaching, and learning suggest that mitigating the weaknesses described, is not only necessary but also possible (Beauchamp & Beauchamp, 2012).

The premise is that nowadays there is less doubt that the education of entrepreneurs could benefit from the intervention of neurosciences. For instance, studies of brain activation can contribute to a more in-depth assessment of the learning processes that an entrepreneur experience (Weigmann, 2013).

If the question is how students develop their entrepreneurial skills (M Lackéus, 2015); if entrepreneurship education is considered to be made up of the content, methods, and activities capable of nurturing student's motivation, skills, and experience to entrepreneuring (Moberg et al., 2014); if the idea is to harmonize entrepreneurial competencies with 21st century skills, such as creativity and critical thinking, then, the disruptive force of neuroscience is nicely inescapable because it has the ability to go deeper to decipher the complexity of cognitive processes of the entrepreneurial brain (Katwala, 2016).

Therefore, the neuro-exploration of the cognitive, affective, and conative processes generated in the entrepreneurial brain can optimize the efficiency of existing pedagogies to learn and teach entrepreneurship (Thrane, Blenker, Korsgaard, & Neergaard, 2016) and add value to what (Loi, Castriotta, & Di Guardo, 2016) call 'training efficiency'.

11.3 Disrupt the design of strategies and policies to support entrepreneurship

Strategies and public policies to promoting entrepreneurship are chiefly comprised of three indicators: outcomes, attitudes, and references (Ács, Autio, & Szerb, 2014). The limitations of these indicators are that they are retrospective and aggregated, making them insufficient for the development of effective policies to support entrepreneurship development.

However, neuroscience can upgrade the efficiency of the formulation of public policies to support entrepreneurship, as it allows the gathering and analysis of higher quality data coming from entrepreneur's brain, in real time, with no intermediaries.

The quality of brain-driven data that could be obtained through the use of neurotechnologies is undeniably a differentiating factor because it could ramp up the effectiveness of policies and strategies (Naudé, 2010) to best support entrepreneurship development, entrepreneurship education, and even boost the improvement of entrepreneurial performance.

It helps that nowadays worldwide decision-makers are in high demand of neuroscience evidence, and scholars are more willing to reflect on the policy implications of their work (Seymour & Vlaev, 2012). For instance, this concurrence of interests between policy design and academia is already occurring in the field of health and social policy (Broer & Pickersgill, 2015), but it is yet pending in entrepreneurship.

The contribution of neuroscience to the determination of more efficient public policies should be prioritized (Seymour & Vlaev, 2012). It is to increase as the gap between empirical evidence and the practical utility of generated evidence closes (Beauchamp & Beauchamp, 2012). It is to gain more accuracy as misapplication, multiple disciplines, language, and knowledge development issues are resolved (Beauchamp & Beauchamp, 2012).

For instance, individual cognitive differences that could make possible to predict which students learn more or less, have already been identified in neuro-education research (Gabrieli, 2016). The elucidation of similar findings is crucial in entrepreneurship as it can stir-up the identification of fitting strategies and public policies to best support entrepreneurship.

11.4 Disrupt the way entrepreneurship is learned

There is no doubt that future entrepreneurs will be trained in laboratories and hospitals. This disruption calls for the neurotechnologies' ability to accelerate the improvement of entrepreneurial performance.

Existing efforts within the arena of entrepreneurship education are focused on training entrepreneurs conventionally. Students of various educational levels are exposed to a variety of training programmes wilfully (aspiring entrepreneurs) or involuntarily to develop their entrepreneurial skills to create and sustain a business.

On the other hand, there are active entrepreneurs who did not go through a formal type of education, the evidence sustains that the outcome of educational effects in this group are also marginal, and little is known about their impact.

The evidence suggests that the impact of entrepreneurship education on active entrepreneurs is contradictory, it still focuses on the intention to start a business rather than on the attained results. There is quantitative data that confirms a positive correlation between education for entrepreneurship and entrepreneurial performance (Martin et al., 2013), but it has also been demonstrated that the effect of education for entrepreneurship analysed in terms of entrepreneurial skills assimilated is insignificant according to students themselves, and the effect of entrepreneurship education on the intention to become an entrepreneur is negative (Oosterbeek, Van Praag, & Ijsselstein, 2010).

This is an area where neuroscience could make a significant input, particularly for the benefit of millions of necessity entrepreneurs who are forced to start businesses but lack the necessary skills (Webb & Fairbourne, 2016) and knowledge (Jeremi, 2014) to move from survival to growth mode (Caliendo & Kritikos, 2010).

It is known that necessity and opportunity entrepreneurs (Cheung, 2014) differ in terms of their cognitive and non-cognitive skills (Calderon & Lacovone, 2017), both are gestated in their brain. The neuroscience strength here is to enlighten novel mechanisms to measure and boost cognitive skills among the wide range of entrepreneurs: entrepreneurship students, aspiring entrepreneurs, necessity, and opportunity entrepreneurs.

Memory, a cognitive skill recognized as critical for entrepreneurial excellence (Baron, 2013), is not the only one that every entrepreneur must cultivate. Good news is that neuroscience can help to strengthen other cognitive functions equally important to the entrepreneur, such as attention, perception, decision-making, processing speed, and reasoning.

Because neurotechnology's can examine how the brain processes information through encoding (what is extracted from available information), retrieval (what is remembered and integrated into understanding), and weighting (what is assigned more or less importance) (Balcetis & Granot, 2015), it has the bona fides to best address the vision of the brain era to entrepreneurship: the acceleration of entrepreneurial performance.

11.5 Disrupt the philosophical grounds of entrepreneurship

Neuroscience's impact on the philosophical grounds of entrepreneurship is imminent, it is to push the update of the ontological, ethical, epistemological, and axiological foundations of the field (Hjorth, 2014; Kurczewska, Kyrö, Lagus, Kohonen, & Lindh-Knuutila, 2017).

This disruption implies transiting from a philosophy of entrepreneurship based on the Continental (Why undertake?) and Anglo-American (What to undertake? and How to undertake?) thinking (Kyrö, 2006) towards one that incorporates the role of neuroscience in the research, teaching, and practice of entrepreneurship.

Currently, there is evidence on epistemological issues (Alvarez & Barney, 2010; Diamond, 2012; George & Marino, 2011; Karatas-Ozkan, Anderson, Fayolle, Howells, & Condor, 2014), ethical principles (Staniewski, Słomski, & Awruk, 2015), and behavioural norms for moral dilemmas in entrepreneurship (Hannafey, 2003), but no further philosophical reflections linked to the influence of neuroscience in the field.

For instance, neurotechnologies are capable of collecting information on brain activity in response to a given stimulus without entering the subconscious or invading an individual's private world or interests (Olteanu, 2015).

Such interventions generate new ethical issues concerning safety, social competence, and human condition improvement (Fuchs, 2006) including the need to take into account additional mechanisms to ensure data protection or dual use (Evers, 2017).

One key question is to what extent is ethical to improve entrepreneurial performance through the manipulation of subjective experiences, cognitive abilities, and personality traits (Fuchs, 2006). These are ethical issues that need to be addressed (Evers, 2017).

Among the myriad of emerging ethical issues arising in the era of the entrepreneurial brain are, three deserve to be prioritized: the implementation of legal mechanisms to regulate the interaction between neuroscience and entrepreneurship at the academia (laws and similar instruments); the establishment of protocols to ensure a proper management of accidental findings and the identification of additional measures to assure the protection of participants before, during, and after an investigation (Olteanu, 2015).

As priorly highlighted, entrepreneurship as a field of scientific research that needs the contribution of neuroscience to cement its legitimacy. The philosophical basis is a critical component in achieving it.

In addition to the disruption of the philosophical underpinnings of entrepreneurship, the remaining four disruptions described in this section have direct ramifications worthy of consideration. The section that follows explores the conceptual, pragmatic, and ethical implications that should be considered as the adoption of a brain-driven approach to entrepreneurship increases over time.

12 Key implications

As one of the primary concerns of the field of entrepreneurship is to advance our understanding of the foundations of entrepreneurial thinking and behaviour (Krueger, 2015), adopting a brain-driven approach as a new paradigm to accelerate the achievement of such a goal necessitates consideration of its implications. This section discusses the conceptual, pragmatic, and ethical implications of the emergence of a brain-driven perspective in the arena of entrepreneurship.

12.1 Conceptual

The book begins by proposing the emergence of a brain-powered era of entrepreneurship, which goes beyond the concept of neuro-entrepreneurship (Foo et al., 2014; Krueger & Welpe, 2014; Shane et al., 2020).

First, the book underlines that neuroscience has shortcomings, but it provides advantages that traditional research methods cannot match. Nevertheless, because brain-driven evidence is difficult to evaluate, it is critical that entrepreneurship scholars learn how to use neuroscience equipment and gain experience in experimental design.

Second, the book investigates the entire range of neuroscience technologies (Kanter, Lykken, Moser, & Moser, 2022). It exposes their flaws and strengths (Zani, Biella, & Proverbio, 2003), and multimodal capabilities (Denison & Morrell, 2022) in order to identify the best technology. The book contributes to the academic community of entrepreneurs by revealing that EEG, ERPs, fMRI, MEG, TMS, tDCS, and neurofeedback are the most promising technologies to test in the field.

It emphasizes in particular the benefits of two technologies for entrepreneurial research, specifically EEG and ERPs. Only EEG can capture data from entrepreneurs' brains on a millisecond scale; no other traditional method can. This is an important contribution because the benefits of EEG

DOI: 10.4324/9781003057109-17

have not been thoroughly discussed in the previous literature (Krueger & Day, 2010).

Third, the book emphasizes that an experimental approach is required for theoretical advancement in the field of entrepreneurship (Hsu et al., 2017; Tan, Fischer, Mitchell, & Phan, 2009; Williams et al., 2019).

The book reveals the experimental principles to consider when approaching an entrepreneurship investigation from a brain-oriented standpoint. It also emphasizes the significance of laboratory experimentation as the best experimental paradigm for entrepreneurship research because it can help to alleviate the most serious constraint to entrepreneurship's legitimacy as a research field: internal validity (Krueger & Welpe, 2014).

Fourth, the book delves into the role of reaction time (RT) to gain a better understanding of decision-making (Lahti, Halko, Karagozoglu, & Wincent, 2019; Laureiro-Martínez et al., 2014; Ortiz-Terán et al., 2014). More concretely, it includes a first exploration of the role of emotional word stimuli in entrepreneurial decision-making using EEG and ERPs technique.

This evidence suggests that using an appropriate experimental design in conjunction with EEG and ERP techniques can reduce methodological constraints (Omorede et al., 2015), mitigate response bias (Furnham, 1986), and contribute to theory development (Kraus et al., 2016). These findings add to the body of knowledge on the topic.

This book also reveals a set of new brain-driven markers for investigating and measuring the relationship between emotions and cognition (N100 and N400).

Because traditional research methods cannot extract, process, and analyse data directly from the entrepreneur's brain (McDonald et al., 2015), neuroscience techniques are now being called upon to meet this challenge. In sum, the book's primary theoretical contribution is the introduction of the fourth era of entrepreneurship, which is distinguished by the use of a brain-driven approach to best measure and improve entrepreneurial performance in venture creation and growth.

12.2 Pragmatic

In keeping with the idea that any entrepreneurship research should produce evidence that extends beyond the scope of entrepreneurship scholars (Shepherd & Wiklund, 2020), this book examined the need of incorporating a brain-driven approach to entrepreneurship from a reflective, theoretical, and empirical viewpoint.

This book will be useful to a wide range of readers, including aspiring entrepreneurs, instructors of entrepreneurship, academics, entrepreneurs, and policymakers. It could, for example, help current and aspiring entrepreneurs learn how brain-driven technologies like EEG and event-related potentials (ERPs) can help them measure the performance of their affective, conative, and cognitive skills, which are critical for entrepreneurial success (Baron, 2013).

The analytical, monitoring, and enhancement capabilities of the neurotechnologies described in the book can benefit entrepreneurs at all stages of development, from conception (decision to start new firm), gestation (decision to start new firm) to inception (new firm born).

Entrepreneurs will gain a better understanding of how a brain-driven oriented view to entrepreneurship can help them better measure and improve their performance, and thus their venture's success. While the consideration of a brain-driven approach to entrepreneuring is not required for every entrepreneur, those who do not consider it as an active success factor of their venture will lose a competitive advantage.

Students studying entrepreneurship at a university will learn and benefit from the ability of neurotechnologies to measure and enhance a variety of affective and cognitive functions crucial to the success of an enterprise.

Policymakers will have access to brand-new, in-depth data extracted directly from the brains of entrepreneurs, which will significantly improve the effectiveness and calibre of their decision-making in support of high-value entrepreneurship.

Higher education institutions can use brain-driven evidence to upgrade the quality and effectiveness of their entrepreneurship education programmes.

Overall, this book offers unique and useful insights for anyone looking to improve their entrepreneurial performance and venture success, which can help usher in a new era of entrepreneurial brain.

12.3 Ethical

A brain-driven research approach to entrepreneurship must adhere to the ethical principles of the Helsinki Declaration (Goodyear, Krleza-Jeric, & Lemmens, 2007), but also to two additional key ethical requirements in order to prioritize participants safety.

The first issue is to consider only non-invasive devices. Non-invasive processes or tests are those that do not necessitate a skin puncture or incision, or the insertion of an instrument or device into the human body. The following technologies are considered non-invasive for entrepreneurship research: EEG, MEG, fMRI, neurofeedback, and tDCS. Among these technologies EEG is the most convenient, safe, and cost-effective device.

The second issue is about unintentional discoveries. A brain-driven entrepreneurship study necessitates the recruitment of human participants as well as the collection of data directly from their brains. It is not uncommon in this framework to discover incidental abnormalities during experimentation. These are purely coincidental findings unrelated to the actual research, but they can be fatal to the participants (Leung, 2013).

It is critical to emphasize that it is always the researcher's responsibility to plan for incidental findings. This can be accomplished by establishing a pathway that allows for timely expert consultation to assess suspicious findings, informing research subjects of the likelihood of incidental findings and consulting on whether participants wish to be contacted, and systematically determining whether individual incidental findings should be disclosed to the participant (Wolf et al., 2008).

The knowledge share thus far has traversed the central elements of this book, beginning with the introduction of the fourth era of entrepreneurship, the key pillars of a brain-driven approach, the identification of appropriate neurotechnologies and themes, and concluding with the disclosure of the key disruptions and repercussions resulting from the progressive adoption of a brain-driven paradigm to entrepreneurship. All of these contributions generate momentum for the following part of the book, in which I discuss the research agenda for the foreseeable future and offer my concluding remarks.

Part VI

Research agenda and final thoughts

13 Research and action agenda for the near future

This research agenda is based on the belief that a brain-driven approach to assessing and enhancing the practice of entrepreneurship is highly needed.

It addresses four pressing issues, all of which aim to elevate the study, teaching, and practice of entrepreneurship to the next level, the brain level. To begin, it is suggested that the scope of research topics under a brain-driven approach be expanded because decision-making is not the only topic that could be investigated using a brain-driven approach. Second, it is suggested that laboratory experimentation be expanded across business schools because it is a natural partner of neurotechnologies. Third, entrepreneurship researchers must quickly learn how to use non-invasive fitting neurotechnologies, because applying the brain-driven approach advocated in this book is impossible without this knowledge and, fourth, in order to accelerate the creation of research synergies, significant efforts should be made to facilitate the formation of a brain-driven research community in the field. The sections that follow go over each of the four mentioned issues in greater detail.

13.1 Extend the scope of brain-driven research

The scope of brain-driven research in entrepreneurship should be expanded. Entrepreneurship scholars are increasingly interested in studying how entrepreneurs think, However, this quest presents methodological constraints (Foo et al., 2014; Omorede et al., 2015; Smith, 2010; Wargo et al., 2010) that conventional methods cannot address.

Neuroscience may be able to assist in addressing this issue in a novel way (Smith, 2010). Neurotechnologies are not without flaws, yet they have the tools and potential to improve our understanding of the entrepreneurial phenomenon (Blair, 2010; de Holan, 2014; Nicolaou & Shane, 2014).

Currently, the state of the art in brain-level entrepreneurship research shows that it is limited to the topic of entrepreneurial decision-making

DOI: 10.4324/9781003057109-19

(Laureiro-Martínez et al., 2014; Ortiz-Terán et al., 2014). This clearly suggests two things. First, the topics to be investigated using a brain-driven approach should be broadened. Second, neurotechnologies can address a wide range of issues (Smith, 2010).

Future research is thus encouraged from four angles. To begin, continue to import and test theories from other fields; there is no need to reinvent the wheel (Landström & Benner, 2010). Entrepreneurship has traditionally drawn on theories from economics, psychology, and sociology (Lohrke & Landström, 2010). It is a beneficial practice (Lohrke & Landström, 2010) because it can lead to the development of one's own unique theories (Zahra, 2007).

Thus, ideas from other neuroscience disciplines such as affective neuroscience, behavioural neuroscience, cultural neuroscience, computational neuroscience, social neuroscience, neuro-informatic, and systems neuroscience should be incorporated. These fields may offer novel frameworks and techniques for investigating a variety of relevant cognitive, conative, affective, and even hormonal and genetic processes (Kurczewska et al., 2017; Nicolaou & Shane, 2014; Toga & Thompson, 2005) that underpin entrepreneurial practice. Furthermore, brain-driven entrepreneurship scholars should be aware that imported theories have been developed to explain different phenomena and, as a result, must be contextualized (Zahra, 2007), because a mismatch between theory and context can lead to inconclusive results (Lohrke & Landström, 2010). Here are some intriguing questions that could benefit from knowledge generated by other branches of neuroscience:

> Throughout the entrepreneurial process, how do entrepreneurs deal with uncertainty and certainty?
> How is the mindset of expert entrepreneurs distinct from that of novices?
> What conative mechanisms are at work before, during, and after the establishment of a venture?
> How do negative emotions, such as failure fear, influence decision-making?

Second, brain-driven entrepreneurship research should be conducted at multiple levels of analysis, particularly at the individual and team levels.

Individual-level research should be prioritized alongside team-level research. Topics such as team interaction (Breugst, Patzelt, & Rathgeber, 2015) and team composition, for example, could benefit greatly from a brain-driven approach, as both influence team and venture success (Knockaert, Ucbasaran, Wright, & Clarysse, 2011). This exercise will necessitate a well-planned experimental design and a clever combination of available brain-imaging tools, but it is certainly feasible. On the other hand, implementing a brain-driven research angle at higher levels, such as firm, industry, population, regional, and national (Davidsson & Wiklund, 2001) may be more difficult. The following are some of the key intriguing questions that should be addressed in this section:

How do emotions like pride, joy, and rage influence entrepreneurial teams' decision-making?

How do executive functions such as memory, perception, and attention affect entrepreneurial team performance?

How does volition work on entrepreneurial teams across the business creation process?

Third, more brain-level research should be done to delve deeper into the decision-making mechanisms that occur during the entrepreneurial process, that is during the business's conception, the event that initiates operations and implementation, and the growth phase (Bygrave, 2009). Exploring the stages of business conceptions and implementation should be given special attention, as current research primarily focuses on entrepreneurs in the growth phase of their businesses (Laureiro-Martínez et al., 2014; Ortiz-Terán et al., 2014).

For instance, the evaluation of entrepreneurs at the stages of idea conception and venture implementation could provide new evidence on the evolution of decision-making as the entrepreneurial process progresses. In this section, one might be interested in using a brain-driven research approach to investigate:

How do cognitive biases influence decision-making during the entrepreneurial process?

What role do schemas play in efficient decision-making during idea generation, implementation, and venture growth?

How do heuristics evolve and influence decision-making across the entrepreneurial process?

How do these processes manifest in the brain?

Fourth, comparative brain-driven research should be conducted on so-called necessity and opportunity entrepreneurs. Necessity entrepreneurs are those who are forced to enter the informal sector due to poverty and unemployment, whereas opportunity entrepreneurs are those who start a formal venture in order to capitalize an innovative business idea (Caliendo & Kritikos, 2010; Cheung, 2014; Desai, 2011; Naudé, 2011).

Brain-based research on these two types of entrepreneurs is strongly encouraged because it may lead to the discovery of relevant cognitive, affective, and conative differences in mindset as well as the discovery of novel neuroscience-based mechanisms to support the mindset shift from necessity to opportunity entrepreneurship, dubbed 'entrepreneurial enhancement' in this book. In light of requests for more brain-driven research on mindset-related issues (McMullen et al., 2014), the following are some intriguing questions pertaining to this topic:

> How do cognition, emotion, and volition interact among necessity and opportunity entrepreneurs?
> Can neurotechnologies be used to train opportunity entrepreneurs?
> How can neurotechnologies be used to improve the well-being and mental health of entrepreneurs?
> How can the mindset shift from necessity to opportunity entrepreneurship be aided?

13.2 Increase laboratory experimentation

The use of experimentation, particularly laboratory experimentation is an essential pillar of a brain-driven research approach. Its use should be expanded across the global community of entrepreneurship scholars for two reasons. For starters, laboratory experimentation can hasten theory generation. It is the most effective way to address methodological and internal validity issues in entrepreneurship research (Foo et al., 2014; Krueger & Welpe, 2014; Omorede et al., 2015).

Existing, and dominant retrospective, self-reporting, and correlational methods do not allow for the establishment of causality and are incapable of collecting data directly from the entrepreneur's brain (Hsu et al., 2017). Only an experiment allows for the plausible determination of causality. Causality testing is important because it can confirm or refute theory-predicted relationships brain (Hsu et al., 2017).

This is a key issue because, due to a lack of theoretical foundation, no widely accepted theory of entrepreneurship has emerged thus far (Binder et al., 2017; Bull & Willard, 1993).

Despite the foregoing, a review of 29 academic entrepreneurship-related journals published between 2000 and 2015 revealed that the number of experimental studies in entrepreneurship remains low brain (Hsu et al., 2017). Only 40 articles with single or multiple designs that used experimental methods were found.

Second, the use of neurotechnologies necessitates the establishment of an experimental setting. The articulation of a well-designed experimental design is undoubtedly the methodological component that precedes the use of any neurotechnology such as EEG and fMRI. Even the most advanced neurotechnology cannot compensate for the flaws of a poor experimental design.

Furthermore, the evidence presented by Hsu et al. (2017) demonstrates the versatility of experimentation to investigate a wide range of topics such as entrepreneurial decision-making, emotions, intentions, opportunities, risk propensity and perception, team dynamics, education, and methodological approaches.

As implied by Shane and Venkataraman (2000), the challenge is to mitigate the view of entrepreneurship as a broad label under which a wide range of research is housed; undoubtedly, the fusion of laboratory experimentation and neurotechnologies can help to address this.

13.3 Incorporate the use of non-invasive fitting neurotechnologies

The use of non-invasive neurotechnologies in the field of entrepreneurship should be encouraged. Future research should specifically aim to increase the individual and combined use of electrophysiological methods like EEG; brain-imaging techniques like fMRI and MEG; brain stimulation tools like tDCS; and novel techniques like neurofeedback, as long as they are preceded by a well-designed experiment.

Here are some examples of intriguing questions that could be addressed using neurotechnologies:

> How neurofeedback could be used to boost entrepreneurial learnings?
> How tDCS could be applied to enhance entrepreneur's cognitive functions such as attention, memory, and decision-making?
> How can neurotechnologies work in tandem with traditional entrepreneurship research methods?

Whatever the case may be, choosing an appropriate neurotechnology should be done with five factors in mind: the type of phenomenon being studied, knowledge of how to use the tool, suitability of the chosen technique, and budget.

13.4 Foster the formation of a brain-driven research community

Future initiatives should encourage the formation of interdisciplinary teams, and university research groups working at the intersection of neuroscience and entrepreneurship. Entrepreneurship research from the brain's perspective is a multidisciplinary endeavour that necessitates expertise from a variety of fields.

In fact, evidence suggests that a brain-driven study requires a high level of interdisciplinary collaboration. These studies typically involve six scholars with expertise in economics, management, neuroscience, technology, psychiatry, and business.

Because conducting research with a brain-driven approach can be challenging for scholars accustomed to traditional research methods, future researchers interested in pursuing a brain-oriented research approach should focus on improving their knowledge of experimental design, cognitive and affective neuroscience, neurotechnologies, data collection techniques, and analysis tools.

The establishment of a vibrant research community motivated by the adoption of a brain-driven approach to the exploration and enhancement of entrepreneurial behaviour is thus critical because it can foster collaboration among scholars from various disciplines, as well as the expansion of research projects, funding, and knowledge exchange.

The first steps have been taken towards establishing a brain-driven research community for entrepreneurship. For example, the Academy of Management has begun organizing a neuro-entrepreneurship symposium, and the WNYLE Institute, a Finland-based Think-Tank focused on entrepreneurship education, has launched a brain-driven training method to nurture and improve the entrepreneurial mindset.

Similar initiatives are expected to emerge as the benefits of this new way of looking at entrepreneurship become known. Meanwhile, the final section of the book contains my closing remarks.

14 Final thoughts

Historically, due to methodological and technological constraints, entrepreneurship has been studied as a static phenomenon. The fourth era of entrepreneurship is introduced in this book as a necessary paradigm shift in response to the need and opportunity to use a brain-driven approach to overcome said constraints and advance our dynamic understanding of entrepreneurship. The new brain-driven paradigm for entrepreneurship repositions the entrepreneur's brain as the central focus of research attention.

We contend that applying a brain-driven paradigm to the field allows for a more in-depth evaluation and enhancement of the entrepreneurial brain's cognitive, affective, and conative functions.

Entrepreneurship is a field that requires immediate theoretical development. It also necessitates the use of latest technologies able to drill down into the apex of entrepreneurial conduct. These constraints can be overcome by utilizing a brain-driven approach based on three components: formulation of an appropriate research question, selection of a fitting neurotechnology, and development of a thorough experimental design.

Things are moving quickly for entrepreneurship students, teachers, researchers, and entrepreneurs these days. Brain-based data collection and analysis could significantly improve the accuracy of entrepreneurship research, teaching, and practice. The brain era will enable the development of tailored neurotherapies aimed at improving not only entrepreneurial performance but also entrepreneurial well-being. Aspiring entrepreneurs and students of entrepreneurship could have early access to these benefits. Teachers of entrepreneurship will acquire a set of new skills to increase their students' chances of entrepreneurial success.

These are significant benefits because a brain-driven approach could be applied to the elucidation of new mechanisms to train, monitor, and improve entrepreneurs' cognitive, affective, and conative performance. The enhancement of these skills is critical for venture success. For instance, the recent introduction of the WNYLE method, a brain-based training

DOI: 10.4324/9781003057109-20

programme designed to strengthen an entrepreneurial mindset, is an excellent illustration of this approach's applicability.

However, the brain era should not be restricted to functional applications like brain mapping or information processing applications like the study of reaction time and event-related potentials. I contend that it should instead be focused on the development of new mechanisms to enhance entrepreneurial performance.

Much more than the separate brain-driven assessment of relevant issues for entrepreneurship described in previous chapters, I advocate that the core target of the brain-driven paradigm is the implementation of enhancement studies on the whole spectrum of affective (anger, passion, joy, and happiness), cognitive (executive processes), and conative (volition) functions at each stage of the venture creation process.

The neurotechnologies behind brain training and brain stimulation are undeniably those that can help improve entrepreneurial performance and entrepreneurs' mental health during business creation in the context of a brain-driven approach. This book embraces this new paradigm as it holds the strengths to disrupt the way entrepreneurship is investigated, taught, learned, promoted, and practiced. In one sentence, a paradigm shift occurs because the conventional way of viewing the world no longer works. We have arrived at this point in the discipline of entrepreneurship.

References

Abutalebi, J., Cappa, S. F., & Perani, D. (2001). The bilingual brain as revealed by functional neuroimaging. *Bilingualism: Language and Cognition, 4*(2), 179–190.

Ács, Z. J., Autio, E., & Szerb, L. (2014). National systems of entrepreneurship: Measurement issues and policy implications. *Research Policy, 43*(3), 476–494.

Aguinis, H., & Lawal, S. O. (2012). Conducting field experiments using eLancing's natural environment. *Journal of Business Venturing, 27*(4), 493–505.

Alain, C., & Winkler, I. (2012). Recording event-related brain potentials: Application to study auditory perception. In D. Poeppel, T. Overath, A. N. Popper, & R. R. Fay (Eds.), *The human auditory cortex* (pp. 69–96). New York: Springer.

Alvarez, S. A., & Barney, J. B. (2010). Entrepreneurship and epistemology: The philosophical underpinnings of the study of entrepreneurial opportunities. *The Academy of Management Annals, 4*(1), 557–583.

Amassian, V. E., Maccabee, P. J., Cracco, R. Q., Cracco, J. B., Rudell, A. P., & Eberle, L. (1993). Measurement of information processing delays in human visual cortex with repetitive magnetic coil stimulation. *Brain Research, 605*(2), 317–321.

Anguera, J., Boccanfuso, J., Rintoul, J., Al-Hashimi, O., Faraji, F., & Janowich, J. (2013). Video game training improves cognitive control in the elderly. *Nature, 501*(7465), 97–101.

Arenius, P., & Minniti, M. (2005). Perceptual variables and nascent entrepreneurship. *Small Business Economics, 24*(3), 233–247.

Ariely, D. (2008). *Predictably irrational: The hidden forces that shape our decisions.* New York, NY: HarperCollins.

Aronson, E., Carlsmith, J. M., & Ellsworth, P. C. (1990). *Methods of research in social psychology* (2nd ed.). New York: McGraw-Hill.

Arpiainen, R.-L., Täks, M., Tynjälä, P., & Lackéus, M. (2013). The sources and dynamics of emotions in entrepreneurship education learning process. *Trames, 17*(4), 331–346.

Ashbridge, E., Walsh, V., & Cowey, A. (1997). Temporal aspects of visual search studied by transcranial magnetic stimulation. *Neuropsychologia, 35*(8), 1121–1131.

Assadollahi, R., & Pulvermüller, F. (2001). Neuromagnetic evidence for early access to cognitive representations. *Neuroreport, 12*(2), 207–213.

Baddeley, A. D. (1997). *Human memory: Theory and practice.* Exeter: Psychology Press.

Bae, T. J., Qian, S., Miao, C., & Fiet, J. O. (2014). The relationship between entrepreneurship education and entrepreneurial intentions: A meta-analytic review. *Entrepreneurship Theory and Practice, 38*(2), 217–254.

Balcetis, E., & Granot, Y. (2015). Under the influence and unaware: Unconscious processing during encoding, retrieval, and weighting in judgment. In G. Keren & G. Wu (Eds.), *The Wiley Blackwell handbook of judgment and decision making* (Vol. 2, pp. 333–355). West Sussex, UK: John Wiley and Sons.

Banich, M. T., & Compton, R. (2011). *Cognitive neuroscience* (3rd ed.). Belmont, CA: Wadsworth Publishing.

Bargh, J. A., & Chartrand, T. L. (2000). The mind in the middle: A practical guide to priming and automaticity research. In H. T. Reis & C. M. Judd (Eds.), *Handbook of research methods in social and personality psychology* (pp. 253–285). New York, NY: Cambridge University Press.

Barkley, R. A. (2001). The executive functions and self-regulation: An evolutionary neuropsychological perspective. *Neuropsychology Review, 11*(1), 1–29.

Baron, R. A. (2008). The role of affect in the entrepreneurial process. *Academy of Management Review, 33*, 328–340.

Baron, R. A. (2013). *Enhancing entrepreneurial excellence: Tools for making the possible real.* Cheltenham, UK: Edward Elgar Publishing, Inc.

Baron, R. A., & Henry, R. A. (2010). How entrepreneurs acquire the capacity to excel: Insights from research on expert performance. *Strategic Entrepreneurship Journal, 4*(1), 49–65.

Baron, R. A., & Ward, T. (2004). Expanding entrepreneurial cognition's toolbox: Potential contributions from the field of cognitive science. *Entrepreneurship Theory and Practice, 28*(6), 553–573.

Bear, M. F., Connors, B. W., & Paradiso, M. A. (2007). *Neuroscience: Exploring the brain* (3rd ed.). Baltimore, MD: Lippincott Williams & Wilkins.

Beauchamp, M., & Beauchamp, C. (2012). Understanding the neuroscience and education connection: Themes emerging from a review of the literature. In S. Della Sala & M. Anderson (Eds.), *Neuroscience in education: The good, the bad, and the ugly* (pp. 13–30). Oxford, UK: Oxford University Press.

Bengtsson, S. L., Dolan, R. J., & Passingham, R. E. (2010). Priming for self-esteem influences the monitoring of one's own performance. *Social Cognitive and Affective Neuroscience, 6*(4), 417–425.

Bernat, E., Bunce, S., & Shevrin, H. (2001). Event-related brain potentials differentiate positive and negative mood adjectives during both supraliminal and subliminal visual processing. *International Journal of Psychophysiology, 42*(1), 11–34.

Beugré, C. D. (2010). Brain and human behavior in organizations: A field of neuro-organizational behavior. In A. A. Stanton, M. Day, & I. M. Welpe (Eds.), *Neuroeconomics and the firm* (pp. 289–303). Cheltenham, UK: Edward Elgar Publishing, Inc.

Binder, J. K., McBride, R., Sud, A., Wuebker, R. J., Krueger, N. F., Cesinger, B., & Pereira, D. (2017). Is "neuroentrepreneurship" worth pursuing? *Academy of Management Proceedings, 2015*(1), 348–361.

Biniari, M. G. (2012). The emotional embeddedness of corporate entrepreneurship: The case of envy. *Entrepreneurship Theory and Practice*, *36*(1), 141–170.

Birley, S., & Westhead, P. (1994). A taxonomy of business start-up reasons and their impact on firm growth and size. *Journal of Business Venturing*, *9*(1), 7–31.

Blair, E. S. (2010). What you think is not what you think: Unconsciousness and entrepreneurial behavior. In A. A. Stanton, M. Day, & I. M. Welpe (Eds.), *Neuroeconomics and the firm* (pp. 50–65). Cheltenham, UK: Edward Elgar Publishing Inc.

Blanchflower, D. G. (2004). Self-employment: More may not be better. *Swedish Economic Policy Review*, *11*(2), 15–74.

Bogacz, R., Wagenmakers, E.-J., Forstmann, B. U., & Nieuwenhuis, S. (2010). The neural basis of the speed: Accuracy tradeoff. *Trends in Neurosciences*, *33*(1), 10–16.

Boggio, P. S., Campanhã, C., Valasek, C. A., Fecteau, S., Pascual-Leone, A., & Fregni, F. (2010). Modulation of decision-making in a gambling task in older adults with transcranial direct current stimulation. *European Journal of Neuroscience*, *31*(3), 593–597.

Bolognini, N., Fregni, F., Casati, C., Olgiati, E., & Vallar, G. (2010). Brain polarization of parietal cortex augments training-induced improvement of visual exploratory and attentional skills. *Brain Research*, *1349*, 76–89.

Boot, W. R., & Kramer, A. F. (2014). The brain-games conundrum: Does cognitive training really sharpen the mind? *Cerebrum: The Dana Forum on Brain Science*, *2014*, 15–15.

BrainWorkshop. (2022). *Brain workshop*.

Brandeis, D., & Lehmann, D. (1986). Event-related potentials of the brain and cognitive processes: Approaches and applications. *Neuropsychologia*, *24*(1), 151–168.

Breugst, N., Patzelt, H., & Rathgeber, P. (2015). How should we divide the pie? Equity distribution and its impact on entrepreneurial teams. *Journal of Business Venturing*, *30*(1), 66–94.

Broer, T., & Pickersgill, M. (2015). Targeting brains, producing responsibilities: The use of neuroscience within British social policy. *Social Science & Medicine*, *132*(May), 54–61.

Broonen, J.-P. (2010). Des intentions aux actes: la volition en conseil en orientation. *L'orientation Scolaire et Professionnelle*, *39*(1), 137–171.

Brundin, E., & Gustafsson, V. (2013). Entrepreneurs' decision making under different levels of uncertainty: The role of emotions. *International Journal of Entrepreneurial Behavior & Research*, *19*, 568–591.

Brunoni, A. R., & Vanderhasselt, M.-A. (2014). Working memory improvement with non-invasive brain stimulation of the dorsolateral prefrontal cortex: A systematic review and meta-analysis. *Brain and Cognition*, *86*(April), 1–9.

Brush, C. G., Manolova, T. S., & Edelman, L. F. (2008). Separated by a common language? Entrepreneurship research across the Atlantic. *Entrepreneurship Theory and Practice*, *32*(2), 249–266.

Bruyat, C., & Julien, P.-A. (2001). Defining the field of research in entrepreneurship. *Journal of Business Venturing*, *16*(2), 165–180.

Buchanan, L., & Connell, A. O. (2006). A brief history of decision making. *Harvard Business Review*, *84*(1), 32–41.

Bull, I., & Willard, G. E. (1993). Towards a theory of entrepreneurship. *Journal of Business Venturing, 8*(3), 183–195.

Bunge, S. A., & Kahn, I. (2009). Cognition: An overview of neuroimaging techniques. In L. H. Squire (Ed.), *Encyclopedia of neuroscience* (Vol. 2, pp. 1063–1067). Oxford, UK: Academic Press.

Burmeister, K., & Schade, C. (2007). Are entrepreneurs' decisions more biased? An experimental investigation of the susceptibility to status quo bias. *Journal of Business Venturing, 22*(3), 340–362.

Bygrave, W. D. (2009). The entrepreneurial process. In W. D. Bygrave & A. Zacharakis (Eds.), *The portable MBA in entrepreneurship* (pp. 1–26). Hoboken: John Wiley & Sons, Inc.

Cabeza, R. (2002). Hemispheric asymmetry reduction in older adults: The HAROLD model. *Psychology and Aging, 17*(1), 85–100.

Cabeza, R., & Nyberg, L. (2000). Imaging cognition II: An empirical review of 275 PET and fMRI studies. *Journal of Cognitive Neuroscience, 12*(1), 1–47.

Cacciotti, G., & Hayton, J. C. (2015). Fear and entrepreneurship: A review and research agenda. *International Journal of Management Reviews, 17*(2), 165–190.

Calderon, G., & Lacovone, L. (2017). Opportunity versus necessity: Understanding the heterogeneity of female micro-entrepreneurs. *World Bank Economic Review, 30*(Supplement 1), 86–96. doi:10.1093/wber/lhw010

Caliendo, M., & Kritikos, A. S. (2010). Start-ups by the unemployed: Characteristics, survival and direct employment effects. *Small Business Economics, 35*(1), 71–92.

Cardon, M. S., Foo, M. D., Shepherd, D., & Wiklund, J. (2012). Exploring the heart: Entrepreneurial emotion is a hot topic. *Entrepreneurship Theory and Practice, 36*, 1–10.

Cardon, M. S., Wincent, J., Singh, J., & Drnovsek, M. (2009). The nature and experience of entrepreneurial passion. *Academy of Management Review, 34*, 511–532.

Carter, M., & Shieh, J. C. (2015). *Guide to research techniques in neuroscience* (2nd ed.). Burlington, MA: Academic Press.

Castillo, E. M., Simos, P. G., Davis, R. N., Breier, J., Fitzgerald, M. E., & Papanicolaou, A. C. (2001). Levels of word processing and incidental memory: Dissociable mechanisms in the temporal lobe. *Neuroreport, 12*(16), 3561–3566.

Cela-Conde, C., Marty, G., Maestú, F., Ortiz, T., Munar, E., Fernández, A., . . . Quesney, F. (2004). Activation of the prefrontal cortex in the human visual aesthetic perception. *Proceedings of the National Academy of Sciences of the United States of America, 101*, 6321–6325.

Charness, G., Gneezy, U., & Kuhn, M. A. (2012). Experimental methods: Between-subject and within-subject design. *Journal of Economic Behavior & Organization, 81*(1), 1–8.

Charron, S., Fuchs, A., & Oullier, O. (2008). Exploring brain activity in neuroeconomics. *Revue d'économie Politique, 118*(1), 97–124.

Cheung, O. L. (2014). Are we seeing "necessity" or "opportunity" entrepreneurs at large? *Research in Business and Economics Journal, 9*(August), 1–26.

Chia, R. (2008). Enhancing entrepreneurial learning through peripheral vision. In R. T. Harrison & C. M. Leitch (Eds.), *Entrepreneurial learning: Conceptual frameworks and applications* (pp. 27–43). London, UK: Routledge.

Chun, M. M., Golomb, J. D., & Turk-Browne, N. B. (2011). A taxonomy of external and internal attention. *Annual Review of Psychology, 62*(1), 73–101.

Clark, V. P., Coffman, B. A., Mayer, A. R., Weisend, M. P., Lane, T. D., Calhoun, V. D., . . . Wassermann, E. M. (2012). tDCS guided using fMRI significantly accelerates learning to identify concealed objects. *Neuroimage, 59*(1), 117–128.

Clarke, J. S., & Cornelissen, J. P. (2014). How language shapes thought: New vistas for entrepreneurship research. In J. R. Mitchell, R. K. Mitchell, & B. Randolph-Seng (Eds.), *Handbook of entrepreneurial cognition* (pp. 383–397). Cheltenham, UK: Edward Elgar Publishing, Inc.

Colquitt, J. A. (2008). From the editors publishing laboratory research in AMJ: A question of when, not if. *Academy of Management Journal, 51*(4), 616–620.

Coolican, H. (2014). *Research methods and statistics in psychology.* Hove, UK: Psychology Press.

Corbett, A., Owen, A., Hampshire, A., Grahn, J., Stenton, R., Dajani, S., . . . Williams, G. (2015). The effect of an online cognitive training package in healthy older adults: An online randomized controlled trial. *Journal of the American Medical Directors Association, 16*(11), 990–997.

Crano, W. D., Brewer, M. B., & Lac, A. (2014). *Principles and methods of social research.* Mahwah, NJ: Lawrence Erlbaum Associates.

Cumming, J., & Williams, S. E. (2012). The role of imagery in performance. In S. M. Murphy (Ed.), *The Oxford handbook of sport and performance psychology* (pp. 213–232). New York: Oxford University Press.

Davidsson, P. (2007). Method challenges and opportunities in the psychological study of entrepreneurship. In B. J. Robert, M. Frese, & R. Baron (Eds.), *The psychology of entrepreneurship* (pp. 287–323). Mahwah, NJ: Lawrence Erlbaum Associates.

Davidsson, P., & Wiklund, J. (2001). Levels of analysis in entrepreneurship research: Current research practice and suggestions for the future. *Entrepreneurship Theory and Practice, 25,* 81–100.

Daw, N. D., O'Doherty, J. P., Dayan, P., Seymour, B., & Dolan, R. J. (2006). Cortical substrates for exploratory decisions in humans. *Nature, 441*(7095), 876–879.

Dayan, E., Censor, N., Buch, E. R., Sandrini, M., & Cohen, L. G. (2013). Noninvasive brain stimulation: From physiology to network dynamics and back. *Nature Neuroscience, 16*(7), 838–844.

De Cock, R., Denoo, L., & Clarysse, B. (2020). Surviving the emotional rollercoaster called entrepreneurship: The role of emotion regulation. *Journal of Business Venturing, 35*(2), 105936.

D'Esposito, M., Postle, B. R., & Rypma, B. (2000). Prefrontal cortical contributions to working memory: Evidence from event-related fMRI studies. *Experimental Brain Research, 133*(1), 3–11.

de Holan, P. M. (2014). It's all in your head: Why we need neuroentrepreneurship. *Journal of Management Inquiry, 23*(1), 93–97.

Delgado García, J. B., De Quevedo Puente, E., & Blanco Mazagatos, V. (2015). How affect relates to entrepreneurship: A systematic review of the literature and research agenda. *International Journal of Management Reviews, 17*(2), 191–211.

Denison, T., & Morrell, M. J. (2022). Neuromodulation in 2035: The neurology future forecasting series. *Neurology, 98*(2), 65–72.

Desai, S. (2011). Measuring entrepreneurship in developing countries. In W. Naudé (Ed.), *Entrepreneurship and economic development* (pp. 94–107). New York, NY: Palgrave Macmillan.

Desmond, J. E., & Glover, G. H. (2002). Estimating sample size in functional MRI (fMRI) neuroimaging studies: Statistical power analyses. *Journal of Neuroscience Methods, 118*(2), 115–128.

Dettmers, S., Trautwein, U., Lüdtke, O., Goetz, T., Frenzel, A. C., & Pekrun, R. (2011). Students' emotions during homework in mathematics: Testing a theoretical model of antecedents and achievement outcomes. *Contemporary Educational Psychology, 36*(1), 25–35.

De Winnaar, K., & Scholtz, F. (2019). Entrepreneurial decision-making: New conceptual perspectives. *Management Decision, 58*(7), 1283–1300.

Diamond, A. M. (2012). The epistemology of entrepreneurship. In R. Koppl & S. Horwitz (Eds.), *Experts and epistemic monopolies* (pp. 111–142). Bingley, UK: Emerald Group Publishing Limited.

Doya, K. (2008). Modulators of decision making. *Nature Neuroscience, 11*(4), 410–416.

Elevate. (2022). *Elevate.* Retrieved from www.elevateapp.com/#/about

Elfenbein, D. W., Hamilton, B. H., & Zenger, T. R. (2010). The small firm effect and the entrepreneurial spawning of scientists and engineers. *Management Science, 56*(4), 659–681.

Evers, K. (2017). The contribution of neuroethics to international brain research initiatives. *Nature Reviews Neuroscience, 18*(1), 1–2.

Eysenck, M. W. (2006). *Fundamentals of cognition.* Hove, UK: Psychology Press.

Eysenck, M. W., & Keane, M. T. (2000). *Cognitive psychology: A student's handbook* (4th ed.). Hove, UK: Psychology Press.

Fauchart, E., & Gruber, M. (2011). Darwinians, communitarians, and missionaries: The role of founder identity in entrepreneurship. *Academy of Management Journal, 54*(5), 935–957.

Fayolle, A. (2013). Personal views on the future of entrepreneurship education. *Entrepreneurship & Regional Development, 25*(7–8), 692–701.

Fernández-Pérez, V., Montes-Merino, A., Rodríguez-Ariza, L., & Galicia, P. E. A. (2019). Emotional competencies and cognitive antecedents in shaping student's entrepreneurial intention: The moderating role of entrepreneurship education. *International Entrepreneurship and Management Journal, 15*(1), 281–305.

FitBrains. (2022). *FitBrains.* Retrieved from www.fitbrains.com/

Fodor, O. C., & Pintea, S. (2017). The "emotional side" of entrepreneurship: A meta-analysis of the relation between positive and negative affect and entrepreneurial performance. *Frontiers in Psychology, 8*, 310.

Foo, M. D. (2011). Emotions and entrepreneurial opportunity evaluation. *Entrepreneurship Theory and Practice, 35*, 375–393.

Foo, M. D., Murnieks, C. Y., & Chan, E. T. (2014). Feeling and thinking: The role of affect in entrepreneurial cognition. In J. R. Mitchell, R. K. Mitchell, & B. Randolph-Seng (Eds.), *Handbook of entrepreneurial cognition* (pp. 154–181). Cheltenham, UK: Edward Elgar Publishing, Inc.

Forlani, D., & Mullins, J. W. (2000). Perceived risks and choices in entrepreneurs' new venture decisions. *Journal of Business Venturing, 15*(4), 305–322.

Friston, K. (2012). Ten ironic rules for non-statistical reviewers. *Neuroimage, 61*(4), 1300–1310.

Fuchs, T. (2006). Ethical issues in neuroscience. *Current Opinion in Psychiatry, 19*(6), 600–607.

Furnham, A. (1986). Response bias, social desirability and dissimulation. *Personality and Individual Differences, 7*(3), 385–400.

Fox, M. D., & Raichle, M. E. (2007). Spontaneous fluctuations in brain activity observed with functional magnetic resonance imaging. *Nature Reviews Neuroscience, 8*(9), 700–711.

Gabrieli, J. D. E. (2016). The promise of educational neuroscience: Comment on Bowers (2016). *Psychological Reviews, 123*(5), 613–619.

Garibotto, V., Borroni, B., Kalbe, E., Herholz, K., Salmon, E., Holtoff, V., . . . Fazio, F. (2008). Education and occupation as proxies for reserve in aMCI converters and AD: FDG-PET evidence. *Neurology, 71*(17), 1342–1349.

Gazzaniga, M. S., Ivry, R. B., & Mangun, G. R. (2014). *Cognitive neuroscience: The biology of the mind* (4th ed.). New York, NY: Norton and Company, Inc.

George, B. A., & Marino, L. (2011). The epistemology of entrepreneurial orientation: Conceptual formation, modeling, and operationalization. *Entrepreneurship Theory and Practice, 35*(5), 989–1024.

Glimcher, P. W., Camerer, C. F., Fehr, E., & Poldrack, R. A. (2009). Introduction: A brief history of neuroeconomics. In P. W. Glimcher, C. F. Camerer, E. Fehr, & R. A. Poldrack (Eds.), *Neuroeconomics: Decision making and the brain* (pp. 1–12). New York: Academic Press.

Goodyear, M. D. E., Krleza-Jeric, K., & Lemmens, T. (2007). The declaration of Helsinki. *BMJ, 335*(7621), 624–625.

Grégoire, D. A., & Lambert, L. S. (2015). Getting inside entrepreneurs' heart and mind: Methods for advancing research on affect and cognition. In T. Baker & F. Welter (Eds.), *The Routledge companion to entrepreneurship* (pp. 450–466). Milton Park, Abingdon: Routledge.

Grichnik, D., Smeja, A., & Welpe, I. (2010). The importance of being emotional: How do emotions affect entrepreneurial opportunity evaluation and exploitation? *Journal of Economic Behavior & Organization, 76*(1), 15–29.

Grühn, D. (2016). An English word database of emotional terms (EMOTE). *Psychological Reports, 119*(1), 290–308.

Gruzelier, J., Foks, M., Steffert, T., Chen, M.-L., & Ros, T. (2014). Beneficial outcome from EEG-neurofeedback on creative music performance, attention and well-being in school children. *Biological Psychology, 95*(January), 86–95.

Hajcak, G., MacNamara, A., & Olvet, D. M. (2010). Event-related potentials, emotion, and emotion regulation: An integrative review. *Developmental Neuropsychology, 35*(2), 129–155.

Hannafey, F. T. (2003). Entrepreneurship and ethics: A literature review. *Journal of Business Ethics, 46*(2), 99–110.

Hayton, J. C., & Cholakova, M. (2012). The role of affect in the creation and intentional pursuit of entrepreneurial ideas. *Entrepreneurship Theory and Practice, 36,* 41–68.

Heinrichs, J.-H. (2012). The promises and perils of non-invasive brain stimulation. *International Journal of Law and Psychiatry, 35*(2), 121–129.

Henry, C., Hill, F., & Leitch, C. (2005). Entrepreneurship education and training: Can entrepreneurship be taught? Part I. *Education and Training, 47*(2), 98–111.

Hernández-Gutiérrez, M. I., & Carrillo-Mora, P. (2017). Aplicaciones terapéuticas de la estimulación cerebral no invasiva en neurorrehabilitación. *Revista Investigación en Discapacidad, 6*(1), 25–33.

Hikkerova, L., Ilouga, S. N., & Sahut, J.-M. (2016). The entrepreneurship process and the model of volition. *Journal of Business Research, 69*(5), 1868–1873.

Hjorth, D. (2014). Sketching a philosophy of entrepreneurship. In T. Baker & F. Welter (Eds.), *The Routledge companion to entrepreneurship* (pp. 41–58). London: Routledge.

Hofmann, W., Schmeichel, B. J., & Baddeley, A. D. (2012). Executive functions and self-regulation. *Trends in Cognitive Sciences, 16*(3), 174–180.

Hoskisson, R. E., Covin, J., Volberda, H. W., & Johnson, R. A. (2011). Revitalizing entrepreneurship: The search for new research opportunities. *Journal of Management Studies, 48,* 1141–1168.

Howard-Jones, P. (2014a). *Neuroscience and education: A review of educational interventions and approaches informed by neuroscience.* Briston: UK: Education Endowment Foundation.

Howard-Jones, P. (2014b). Neuroscience and education: Myths and messages. *Nature Reviews Neuroscience, 15*(December), 817–824.

Hsu, D. K., Simmons, S. A., & Wieland, A. M. (2017). Designing entrepreneurship experiments: A review, typology, and research agenda. *Organizational Research Methods, 20*(3), 379–412.

Huettel, S., Song, A., & McCarthy, G. (2009). *Functional magnetic resonance imaging* (2nd ed.). Sunderland, MA: Sinauer Associates.

Hyer, L., Scott, C., Atkinson, M. M., Mullen, C. M., Lee, A., Johnson, A., & Mckenzie, L. C. (2016). Cognitive training program to improve working memory in older adults with MCI. *Clinical Gerontologist, 39*(5), 410–427.

Illes, J., Desmond, J. E., Huang, L. F., Raffin, T. A., & Atlas, S. W. (2002). Ethical and practical considerations in managing incidental findings in functional magnetic resonance imaging. *Brain and Cognition, 50*(3), 358–365.

Illes, J., Kirschen, M. P., Edwards, E., Stanford, L. R., Bandettini, P., Cho, M. K., . . . Macklin, R. (2006). Incidental findings in brain imaging research: What should happen when a researcher sees a potential health problem in a brain scan from a research subject? *Science, 311*(5762), 783–784.

Jack, S. L. (2010). Approaches to studying networks: Implications and outcomes. *Journal of Business Venturing, 25*(1), 120–137.

Jeremi, B. (2014). Defining and classifying necessity entrepreneurs: A review of the literature. In J. Brewer & S. W. Gibson (Eds.), *Necessity entrepreneurs:*

Microenterprise education and economic development (pp. 1–22). Cheltenham, UK: Edward Elgar Publishing, Inc.

Jones, S., & Underwood, S. (2017). Understanding students' emotional reactions to entrepreneurship education: A conceptual framework. *Education+ Training, 59*(7/8), 657–671.

Kandel, E. R., Schwartz, J. H., & Jessell, T. M. (2000). *Principles of neural science.* New York: McGraw-Hill.

Kanter, B. R., Lykken, C. M., Moser, E. I., & Moser, M.-B. (2022). Neuroscience in the 21st century: Circuits, computation, and behaviour. *The Lancet Neurology, 21*(1), 19–21.

Kappenman, E. S., & Luck, S. J. (2010). The effects of electrode impedance on data quality and statistical significance in ERP recordings. *Psychophysiology, 47*(5), 888–904.

Karatas-Ozkan, M., Anderson, A. R., Fayolle, A., Howells, J., & Condor, R. (2014). Understanding entrepreneurship: Challenging dominant perspectives and theorizing entrepreneurship through new postpositivist epistemologies. *Journal of Small Business Management, 52*(4), 589–593.

Kass, R. E., Eden, U. T., & Brown, E. N. (2014). *Analysis of neural data.* New York: Springer.

Katwala, A. (2016). *The athletic brain: How neuroscience is revolutionising sport and can help you perform better.* London, UK: Simon and Schuster.

Katzman, G. L., Dagher, A. P., & Patronas, N. J. (1999). Incidental findings on brain magnetic resonance imaging from 1000 asymptomatic volunteers. *Jama, 282*(1), 36–39.

Kiely, K. M. (2014). Cognitive function. In A. C. Michalos (Ed.), *Encyclopedia of quality of life and well-being research* (pp. 974–978). Dordrecht: Springer.

Kincses, T. Z., Antal, A., Nitsche, M. A., Bártfai, O., & Paulus, W. (2004). Facilitation of probabilistic classification learning by transcranial direct current stimulation of the prefrontal cortex in the human. *Neuropsychologia, 42*(1), 113–117.

Klapproth, F. (2008). Time and decision making in humans. *Cognitive, Affective & Behavioral Neuroscience, 8*(4), 509–524.

Klimova, B. (2016). Computer-based cognitive training in aging. *Frontiers in Aging Neuroscience, 8*.

Knockaert, M., Ucbasaran, D., Wright, M., & Clarysse, B. (2011). The relationship between knowledge transfer, top management team composition, and performance: The case of science-based entrepreneurial firms. *Entrepreneurship Theory and Practice, 35*(4), 777–803.

Koizumi, A., Amano, K., Cortese, A., Shibata, K., Yoshida, W., Seymour, B., . . . Lau, H. (2016). Fear reduction without fear through reinforcement of neural activity that bypasses conscious exposure. *Nature Human Behaviour, 1*, 0006.

Kolling, N., Wittmann, M., & Rushworth, M. F. (2014). Multiple neural mechanisms of decision making and their competition under changing risk pressure. *Neuron, 81*(5), 1190–1202.

Kraus, S., Meier, F., & Niemand, T. (2016). Experimental methods in entrepreneurship research: The status quo. *International Journal of Entrepreneurial Behavior & Research, 22*(6), 958–983.

Krueger, N. (2015). The entrepreneurial mindset. In V. K. Gupta, D. K. Dutta, C. G. Guo, A. E. Osorio, & B. Ozkazanc-Pan (Eds.), *Foundational research in entrepreneurship studies: Insightful contributions and future pathways*. Cham, Switzerland: Palgrave Macmillan.

Krueger, N., & Day, M. (2010). Looking forward, looking backward: From entrepreneurial cognition to neuroentrepreneurship. In Z. J. Acs & D. B. Audretsch (Eds.), *Handbook of entrepreneurship research* (pp. 321–357). New York: Springer.

Krueger, N., & Welpe, I. (2008, January 10–13). *Experimental entrepreneurship: A research prospectus and workshop*. Paper presented at the USASBE Annual Conference, San Antonio, TX.

Krueger, N., & Welpe, I. (2014). Neuroentrepreneurship: What can entrepreneurship learn from neuroscience? In M. H. Morris (Ed.), *Annals of entrepreneurship education and pedagogy* (pp. 60–90). Cheltenham, UK: Edward Elgar Publishing, Inc.

Kueider, A. M., Parisi, J. M., Gross, A. L., & Rebok, G. W. (2012). Computerized cognitive training with older adults: A systematic review. *PLoS One, 7*(7), e40588.

Kurczewska, A., Kyrö, P., Lagus, K., Kohonen, O., & Lindh-Knuutila, T. (2017). The interplay between cognitive, conative, and affective constructs along the entrepreneurial learning process. *Education+ Training*.

Kyrö, P. (2006). The continental and Anglo-American approaches to entrepreneurship education, differences and bridges. In F. A & K. H (Eds.), *International entrepreneurship education, issues and newness* (pp. 93–111). Cheltenham UK: Edward Elgar Publishing Inc.

LaBar, K. S., Gitelman, D. R., Parrish, T. B., & Mesulam, M.-M. (1999). Neuroanatomic overlap of working memory and spatial attention networks: A functional MRI comparison within subjects. *Neuroimage, 10*(6), 695–704.

Lackéus, M. (2014). An emotion based approach to assessing entrepreneurial education. *The International Journal of Management Education, 12*(3), 374–396.

Lackéus, M. (2015). Entrepreneurship in education: What, why, when, how. In *Entrepreneurship 360 background paper*. Paris: OECD Publishing.

Lahti, T., Halko, M.-L., Karagozoglu, N., & Wincent, J. (2019). Why and how do founding entrepreneurs bond with their ventures? Neural correlates of entrepreneurial and parental bonding. *Journal of Business Venturing, 34*(2), 368–388.

Lamers, M. J., Roelofs, A., & Rabeling-Keus, I. M. (2010). Selective attention and response set in the Stroop task. *Memory & Cognition, 38*(7), 893–904.

Lampit, A., Hallock, H., & Valenzuela, M. (2014). Computerized cognitive training in cognitively healthy older adults: A systematic review and meta-analysis of effect modifiers. *PLoS Medicine, 11*(11).

Landström, H. (2004). Pioneers in entrepreneurship research. In G. Corbetta, M. Huse, & D. Ravasi (Eds.), *Crossroads of entrepreneurship* (pp. 13–32). Dordrecht: Kluwer Academic Publishers.

Landström, H. (2007). *Pioneers in entrepreneurship and small business research*. New York: Springer.

Landström, H., & Benner, M. (2010). Entrepreneurship research: A history of scholarly migration. In H. Landström & F. Lohrke (Eds.), *Historical foundations of entrepreneurship research* (pp. 15–45). Cheltenham, UK: Edward Elgar Publishing, Inc.

Laureiro-Martínez, D., Canessa, N., Brusoni, S., Zollo, M., Hare, T., Alemanno, F., & Cappa, S. (2014). Frontopolar cortex and decision-making efficiency: Comparing brain activity of experts with different professional background during an exploration-exploitation task. *Frontiers in Human Neuroscience*, 7(927), 1–10.

Laureiro-Martinez, D., Venkatraman, V., Cappa, S., Zollo, M., & Brusoni, S. (2015). Cognitive neurosciences and strategic management: Challenges and opportunities in tying the knot. In G. Gavetti & W. Ocasio (Eds.), *Cognition and strategy* (Vol. 32, pp. 351–370). Bingley, UK: Emerald Group Publishing Limited.

Lerner, J. S., Li, Y., Valdesolo, P., & Kassam, K. S. (2015). Emotion and decision making. *Psychology*, 66.

Leung, L. (2013). Incidental findings in neuroimaging: Ethical and medicolegal considerations. *Neuroscience Journal*, 2013.

Levitin, D. J. (2002). *Foundations of cognitive psychology: Core readings*. Cambridge, MA: MIT Press.

Lewis, P. M., Thomson, R. H., Rosenfeld, J. V., & Fitzgerald, P. B. (2016). Brain neuromodulation techniques: A review. *The Neuroscientist*, 22(4), 406–421.

Logan, G. D. (2008). The role of memory in the control of action. In M. E., B. J. A., & G. P. M. (Eds.), *The Oxford handbook of human action* (pp. 427–441). Oxford, UK: Oxford University Press.

Logothetis, N. K. (2008). What we can do and what we cannot do with fMRI. *Nature*, 453(7197), 869–878.

Lohrke, F., & Landström, H. (2010). History matters in entrepreneurship research. In F. Lohrke & H. Landström (Eds.), *Historical foundations of entrepreneurship research* (pp. 1–11). Cheltenham: Edward Elgar Publishing Inc.

Loi, M., Castriotta, M., & Di Guardo, M. C. (2016). The theoretical foundations of entrepreneurship education: How co-citations are shaping the field. *International Small Business Journal*, 34(7), 948–971.

Luck, S. J. (2014). *An introduction to the event-related potential technique* (2nd ed.). Cambridge, MA: MIT Press.

Lumosity. (2022). *Lumosity*. Retrieved from www.lumosity.com/about

Maine, E., Soh, P.-H., & Dos Santos, N. (2015). The role of entrepreneurial decision-making in opportunity creation and recognition. *Technovation*, 39–40(May–June), 53–72.

Mark, M. M., & Reichardt, C. S. (2004). Quasi-experimental and correlational designs: Methods for the real world when random assignment isn't feasible. In C. Sansone, C. C. Morf, & A. T. Panter (Eds.), *The Sage handbook of methods in social psychology* (pp. 265–286). Thousand Oaks, CA: Sage Publications, Inc.

Martin, B. C., McNally, J. J., & Kay, M. J. (2013). Examining the formation of human capital in entrepreneurship: A meta-analysis of entrepreneurship education outcomes. *Journal of Business Venturing*, 28(2), 211–224.

Mather, M., Cacioppo, J. T., & Kanwisher, N. (2013). How fMRI can inform cognitive theories. *Perspectives on Psychological Science*, 8(1), 108–113.

Maxwell, S. E., Delaney, H. D., & Kelley, K. (2017). *Designing experiments and analyzing data: A model comparison perspective*. New York: Routledge.

McAvinue, L. P., Golemme, M., Castorina, M., Tatti, E., Pigni, F. M., Salomone, S., . . . Robertson, I. H. (2013). An evaluation of a working memory training scheme in older adults. *Frontiers in Aging Neuroscience, 5*, 20.

McBride, R. (2015). The hidden complexities of "entrepreneurial opportunity". *Academy of Management Proceedings, 2015*(1), 155–156.

McDonald, S., Gan, B. C., Fraser, S. S., Oke, A., & Anderson, A. R. (2015). A review of research methods in entrepreneurship 1985–2013. *International Journal of Entrepreneurial Behavior & Research, 21*(3), 291–315.

Mcintosh, A. R. (1998). Understanding neural interactions in learning and memory using functional neuroimaging. *Annals of the New York Academy of Sciences, 855*(1), 556–571.

McMullen, J. S., Wood, M. S., & Palich, L. E. (2014). Entrepreneurial cognition and social cognitive neuroscience. In J. R. Mitchell, R. K. Mitchell, & B. Randolph-Seng (Eds.), *Handbook of entrepreneurial cognition*. Cheltenham, UK: Edward Elgar Publishing Inc.

McVea, J. F. (2009). A field study of entrepreneurial decision-making and moral imagination. *Journal of Business Venturing, 24*(5), 491–504.

Melby-Lervåg, M., & Hulme, C. (2013). Is working memory training effective? A meta-analytic review. *Developmental Psychology, 49*(2), 270–291.

Michl, T., Welpe, I. M., Spörrle, M., & Picot, A. (2009). The role of emotions and cognitions in entrepreneurial decision-making. In L. A. Carsrud & M. Brännback (Eds.), *Understanding the entrepreneurial mind* (pp. 167–190). Heidelberg: Springer.

Minati, L., Campanha, C., Critchley, H. D., & Boggio, P. S. (2012). Effects of transcranial direct-current stimulation (tDCS) of the dorsolateral prefrontal cortex (DLPFC) during a mixed-gambling risky decision-making task. *Cognitive Neuroscience, 3*(2), 80–88.

Miniussi, C., Harris, J. A., & Ruzzoli, M. (2013). Modelling non-invasive brain stimulation in cognitive neuroscience. *Neuroscience & Biobehavioral Reviews, 37*(8), 1702–1712.

Mitchell, R. K., Busenitz, L., Bird, B., Gaglio, M., McMullen, J., Morse, E., & Smith, B. (2007). The central question in entrepreneurial cognition research 2007. *Entrepreneurship Theory and Practice, 31*(1), 1–27.

Mitteness, C., Sudek, R., & Cardon, M. S. (2012). Angel investor characteristics that determine whether perceived passion leads to higher evaluations of funding potential. *Journal of Business Venturing, 27*, 592–606.

Moberg, K., Vestergaard, L., Fayolle, A., Redford, D., Cooney, T., Singer, S., . . . Filip, D. (2014). *How to assess and evaluate the influence of entrepreneurship education: A report of the ASTEE project with a user guide to the tools*. Odense: The Danish Foundation for Entrepreneurship – Young Enterprise.

Mook, D. G. (1983). In defense of external invalidity. *American Psychologist, 38*(4), 379–387.

Morris, H. M., Pryor, G. C., & Schindehutte, M. (2012). *Entrepreneurship as experience: How events create ventures and ventures create entrepreneurs*. Cheltenham, UK: Edward Elgar Publishing Inc.

Nabi, G., Liñán, F., Fayolle, A., Krueger, N., & Walmsley, A. (2016). The impact of entrepreneurship education in higher education: A systematic review and research agenda. *Academy of Management Learning & Education, 16*(2), 277–299.

Naudé, W. (2010). *Promoting entrepreneurship in developing countries: Policy challenges Policy Brief 04*. Helsinki: World Institute for Development Economics Research.

Naudé, W. (2011). Entrepreneurship is not a binding constraint on growth and development in the poorest countries. *World Development, 39*(1), 33–44.

Nelson, C. A. (2008). Incidental findings in magnetic resonance imaging (MRI) brain research. *The Journal of Law, Medicine & Ethics, 36*(2), 315–319.

Neugebauer, E., Rothmund, M., & Lorenz, W. (1989). The concept, structure and practice of prospective clinical studies. *Zeitschrift für alle Gebiete der Operativen Medizen, 60*(4), 203–213.

Nicolaou, N., & Shane, S. (2014). Biology, neuroscience, and entrepreneurship. *Journal of Management Inquiry, 23,* 98–100.

Nieto, M. A. P., Fernández-Abascal, E. G., & Miguel-Tobal, J. J. (2009). The role of emotions in decision-making. *Studia Psychologica, 51*(4), 305.

Nitsche, M. A., Kuo, M.-F., Paulus, W., & Antal, A. (2015). Transcranial direct current stimulation: Protocols and physiological mechanisms of action. In H. Knotkova & D. Rasche (Eds.), *Textbook of neuromodulation: Principles, methods and clinical applications* (pp. 101–111). New York, NY: Springer.

Nitsche, M. A., & Paulus, W. (2011). Transcranial direct current stimulation – update 2011. *Restorative Neurology and Neuroscience, 29*(6), 463–492.

Nordqvist, C. (2014, September 26). What is neuroscience? *Medical News Today*. Retrieved from www.medicalnewstoday.com/

Norris, C. J., Coan, J. A., & Johnstone, T. (2007). Functional magnetic resonance imaging and the study of emotion. In J. A. Coan & J. J. B. Allen (Eds.), *Handbook of emotion elicitation and assessment* (pp. 440–459). Oxford, UK: Oxford University Press.

Olteanu, M. D. B. (2015). Neuroethics and responsibility in conducting neuromarketing research. *Neuroethics, 8*(2), 191–202.

Omorede, A., Thorgren, S., & Wincent, J. (2015). Entrepreneurship psychology: A review. *International Entrepreneurship and Management Journal, 11*(4), 743–768.

Oosterbeek, H., Van Praag, M., & Ijsselstein, A. (2010). The impact of entrepreneurship education on entrepreneurship skills and motivation. *European Economic Review, 54*(3), 442–454.

Ortiz-Terán, E., Turrero, A., Santos, J. M., Bryant, P. T., Ortiz, T., Ortiz-Terán, E., . . . Ortiz, T. (2014). Brain cortical organization in entrepreneurs during a visual Stroop decision task. *Clinical, Cosmetic and Investigational Dentistry, 6,* 45–56.

Ouellet, J., McGirr, A., Van den Eynde, F., Jollant, F., Lepage, M., & Berlim, M. T. (2015). Enhancing decision-making and cognitive impulse control with transcranial direct current stimulation (tDCS) applied over the orbitofrontal cortex (OFC): A randomized and sham-controlled exploratory study. *Journal of Psychiatric Research, 69*(October), 27–34.

Parkes, L., Perry, C., & Goodin, P. (2016). Examining the N400m in affectively negative sentences: A magnetoencephalography study. *Psychophysiology, 53*(5), 689–704.

Pascual-Leone, A., Grafman, J., & Hallett, M. (1994). Modulation of cortical motor output maps during development of implicit and explicit knowledge. *Science, 263*(5151), 1287–1289.

Patel, P. C., & Fiet, J. O. (2010). Enhancing the internal validity of entrepreneurship experiments by assessing treatment effects at multiple levels across multiple trials. *Journal of Economic Behavior & Organization, 76,* 127–140.

Pekrun, R., Goetz, T., Frenzel, A. C., Barchfeld, P., & Perry, R. P. (2011). Measuring emotions in students' learning and performance: The Achievement Emotions Questionnaire (AEQ). *Contemporary Educational Psychology, 36*(1), 36–48.

Pérez-Centeno, V. (2017). Brain-driven entrepreneurship research: A review and research agenda. In M. Day, M. Boardman, & K. Norris (Eds.), *Handbook of research methodologies and design in neuro-entrepreneurship.* Cheltenham, UK: Edward Elgar Publishing Inc.

Picton, T., & Hillyard, S. (1972). Cephalic skin potentials in electroencephalography. *Electroencephalography and Clinical Neurophysiology, 33*(4), 419–424.

Pittaway, L., & Cope, J. (2007). Simulating entrepreneurial learning: Integrating experiential and collaborative approaches to learning. *Management Learning, 38*(2), 211–233.

Pless, N. M., Maak, T., & Stahl, G. K. (2011). Developing responsible global leaders through international service-learning programs: The Ulysses experience. *Academy of Management Learning & Education, 10*(2), 237–260.

Poldrack, R. A. (2006). Can cognitive processes be inferred from neuroimaging data? *Trends in Cognitive Sciences, 10*(2), 59–63.

Poldrack, R. A. (2011). Inferring mental states from neuroimaging data: From reverse inference to large-scale decoding. *Neuron, 72*(5), 692–697.

Pripfl, J., Neumann, R., Köhler, U., & Lamm, C. (2013). Effects of transcranial direct current stimulation on risky decision making are mediated by "hot" and "cold" decisions, personality, and hemisphere. *European Journal of Neuroscience, 38*(12), 3778–3785.

Pushkarskaya, H., Smithson, M., Liu, X., & Joseph, J. E. (2010). Neuroeconomics of environmental uncertainty and the theory of the firm. In A. A. Stanton, M. Day, & I. M. Welpe (Eds.), *Neuroeconomics and the firm* (pp. 13–28). Cheltenham, UK: Edward Elgar Publishing Inc.

Rabipour, S., & Raz, A. (2012). Training the brain: Fact and fad in cognitive and behavioral remediation. *Brain and Cognition, 79*(2), 159–179.

Rahmati, N., Rostami, R., Zali, M. R., Nowicki, S., & Zarei, J. (2014). The effectiveness of neurofeedback on enhancing cognitive process involved in entrepreneurship abilities among primary school students in district No. 3 Tehran. *Basic and Clinical Neuroscience, 5*(4), 277–284.

Rämä, P., Martinkauppi, S., Linnankoski, I., Koivisto, J., Aronen, H. J., & Carlson, S. (2001). Working memory of identification of emotional vocal expressions: An fMRI study. *Neuroimage, 13*(6), 1090–1101.

Roberts, T. P., Ferrari, P., Perry, D., Rowley, H. A., & Berger, M. S. (2000). Presurgical mapping with magnetic source imaging: Comparisons with intraoperative findings. *Brain Tumor Pathology, 17*(2), 57–64.

Röhrig, B., du Prel, J.-B., Wachtlin, D., & Blettner, M. (2009). Types of study in medical research: Part 3 of a series on evaluation of scientific publications. *Deutsches Arzteblatt International, 106*(15), 262–268.

Rolls, E. T. (2014). *Emotion and decision-making explained.* Oxford: Oxford University Press.

Rolls, E. T., & Treves, A. (2011). The neuronal encoding of information in the brain. *Progress in Neurobiology, 95*(3), 448–490.

Rossi, S., Hallett, M., Rossini, P. M., Pascual-Leone, A., & Group, S. o. T. C. (2009). Safety, ethical considerations, and application guidelines for the use of transcranial magnetic stimulation in clinical practice and research. *Clinical Neurophysiology, 120*(12), 2008–2039.

Ruff, C. C., & Huettel, S. A. (2014). Experimental methods in cognitive neuroscience. In P. W. Glimcher & E. Fehr (Eds.), *Neuroeconomics: Decision making and the Brain* (2nd ed., pp. 77–108). San Diego, CA: Academic Press.

Schacter, D. L., Gilbert, D. T., Nock, M., & Wegner, D. M. (2020). *Psychology.* New York, NY: Worth Publishers, Macmillan Learning.

Schade, C. (2005). Dynamics, experimental economics, and entrepreneurship. *The Journal of Technology Transfer, 30,* 409–431.

Schade, C., & Burmeister, K. (2009). Experiments on entrepreneurial decision making: A different lens through which to look at entrepreneurship. *Foundations and Trends in Entrepreneurship, 5*(2), 81–134.

Schulte-Rüther, M., Markowitsch, H. J., Shah, N. J., Fink, G. R., & Piefke, M. (2008). Gender differences in brain networks supporting empathy. *Neuroimage, 42*(1), 393–403.

Seymour, B., & Vlaev, I. (2012). Can, and should, behavioural neuroscience influence public policy? *Trends in Cognitive Sciences, 16*(9), 449–451.

Shane, S. (2003). *A general theory of entrepreneurship: The individual-opportunity nexus.* Aldershot, UK: Edward Elgar.

Shane, S., Drover, W., Clingingsmith, D., & Cerf, M. (2020). Founder passion, neural engagement and informal investor interest in startup pitches: An fMRI study. *Journal of Business Venturing, 35*(4), 105949.

Shane, S., & Venkataraman, S. (2000). The promise of entrepreneurship as a field of research. *Academy of Management Review, 25*(1), 217–226.

Shaver, K. G. (2014). Experimental methods in entrepreneurship research. In A. L. Carsrud & M. Brännback (Eds.), *Handbook of research methods and applications in entrepreneurship and small business* (pp. 88–111). Cheltenham, UK: Edward Elgar Publishing Inc.

Shepherd, D. A., & Patzelt, H. (2015). The "heart" of entrepreneurship: The impact of entrepreneurial action on health and health on entrepreneurial action. *Journal of Business Venturing Insights, 4,* 22–29.

Shepherd, D. A., & Patzelt, H. (2018). *Entrepreneurial cognition: Exploring the mindset of entrepreneurs* Basingstock: Springer Nature.

Shepherd, D. A., & Wiklund, J. (2020). Simple rules, templates, and heuristics! An attempt to deconstruct the craft of writing an entrepreneurship paper. *Entrepreneurship Theory and Practice, 44*(3), 371–390.

Shepherd, D. A., Williams, T. A., & Patzelt, H. (2015). Thinking about entrepreneurial decision making review and research agenda. *Journal of Management, 41*(1), 11–46.

Sitaram, R., Ros, T., Stoeckel, L., Haller, S., Scharnowski, F., Lewis-Peacock, J., ... Oblak, E. (2016). Closed-loop brain training: The science of neurofeedback. *Nature Reviews Neuroscience, 18*(February), 86–100.

Smith, R. (2010). Mapping neurological drivers to entrepreneurial proclivity. In S. A. A., D. Mellani, & W. I. M. (Eds.), *Neuroeconomics and the firm* (pp. 193–216). Cheltenham, UK: Edward Elgar Publishing Inc.

Souitaris, V., Zerbinati, S., & Al-Laham, A. (2007). Do entrepreneurship programmes raise entrepreneurial intention of science and engineering students? The effect of learning, inspiration and resources. *Journal of Business Venturing, 22*(4), 566–591.

Spezio, M. L., & Adolphs, R. (2010). Emotion, cognition, and belief findings from cognitive neuroscience. In B. Tim & F. Jordi (Eds.), *Delusion and self-deception: Affective and motivational influences on belief formation* (1st ed., pp. 87–105). New York, NY: Psychology Press.

Stagg, C. J., & Nitsche, M. A. (2011). Physiological basis of transcranial direct current stimulation. *The Neuroscientist, 17*(1), 37–53.

Staniewski, M. W., Słomski, W., & Awruk, K. (2015). Ethical aspects of entrepreneurship. *Filosofija Sociologija, 1*, 37–45.

Stefan, K., Kunesch, E., Cohen, L. G., Benecke, R., & Classen, J. (2000). Induction of plasticity in the human motor cortex by paired associative stimulation. *Brain, 123*(3), 572–584.

Symmonds, M., Moran, R. J., Wright, N. D., Bossaerts, P., Barnes, G., & Dolan, R. J. (2013). The chronometry of risk processing in the human cortex. *Frontiers in Neuroscience, 7*, 146.

Tan, J., Fischer, E., Mitchell, R. K., & Phan, P. (2009). At the center of the action: Innovation and technology strategy research in the small business setting. *Journal of Small Business Management, 47*(3), 233–262.

Tata, A., Martinez, D. L., Garcia, D., Oesch, A., & Brusoni, S. (2017). The psycholinguistics of entrepreneurship. *Journal of Business Venturing Insights, 7*, 38–44.

Thiese, M. S. (2014). Observational and interventional study design types; an overview. *Biochemia Medica, 24*(2), 199–210.

Thrane, C., Blenker, P., Korsgaard, S., & Neergaard, H. (2016). The promise of entrepreneurship education: Reconceptualizing the individual – opportunity nexus as a conceptual framework for entrepreneurship education. *International Small Business Journal, 34*(7), 905–924.

Toga, A. W., & Thompson, P. M. (2005). Genetics of brain structure and intelligence. *Annual Review of Neuroscience, 28*(1), 1–23.

Tracey, P., & Schluppeck, D. (2014). Neuroentreprenuership: "Brain pornography" or new frontier in entrepreneurship research? *Journal of Management Inquiry, 23*(1), 101–103.

Treffers, T., Welpe, I., Spörrle, M., & Picot, A. (2017). The role of emotions and cognitions in the pre-entrepreneurial process: What's new? In A. A. Stanton, M.

Day, & I. M. Welpe (Eds.), *Neuroeconomics and the firm* (pp. 50–65). Cheltenham, UK: Edward Elgar Publishing Inc.

Trochim, W. M. (2001). *Research methods knowledge base* (2nd ed.). Cincinnati, OH: Atomic Dog.

Tully, L. M., & Boudewyn, M. A. (2018). *Creating a novel experimental paradigm: A practical guide.* London: SAGE Publications Ltd.

van't Wout, M., Kahn, R. S., Sanfey, A. G., & Aleman, A. (2005). Repetitive transcranial magnetic stimulation over the right dorsolateral prefrontal cortex affects strategic decision-making. *Neuroreport, 16*(16), 1849–1852.

Veniero, D., Strüber, D., Thut, G., & Herrmann, C. S. (2016). Noninvasive brain stimulation techniques can modulate cognitive processing. *Organizational Research Methods 22*(1), 116–147.

Venkatraman, V., Huettel, S. A., Chuah, L. Y., Payne, J. W., & Chee, M. W. (2011). Sleep deprivation biases the neural mechanisms underlying economic preferences. *The Journal of Neuroscience, 31*(10), 3712–3718.

Venkatraman, V., Rosati, A. G., Taren, A. A., & Huettel, S. A. (2009). Resolving response, decision, and strategic control: Evidence for a functional topography in dorsomedial prefrontal cortex. *The Journal of Neuroscience, 29*(42), 13158–13164.

Wagner, T., Valero-Cabre, A., & Pascual-Leone, A. (2007). Noninvasive human brain stimulation. *Annual Review of Biomedical Engineering, 9,* 527–565.

Walsh, V., & Cowey, A. (1998). Magnetic stimulation studies of visual cognition. *Trends in Cognitive Sciences, 2*(3), 103–110.

Walsh, V., & Cowey, A. (2000). Transcranial magnetic stimulation and cognitive neuroscience. *Nature Reviews Neuroscience, 1*(1), 73–80.

Walton, C. C., Kavanagh, A., Downey, L. A., Lomas, J., Camfield, D. A., & Stough, C. (2015). Online cognitive training in healthy older adults: A preliminary study on the effects of single versus multi-domain training. *Translational Neuroscience, 6*(1), 13–19.

Wargo, D. T., Baglini, N. A., & Nelson, K. A. (2010). What neuroeconomics informs us about making real-world ethical decisions in organizations. In A. A. Stanton, M. Day, & I. M. Welpe (Eds.), *Neuroeconomics and the firm* (pp. 235–262). Cheltenham, UK: Edward Elgar Publishing Inc.

Webb, P., & Fairbourne, J. (2016). Microfranchising: A solution to necessity entrepreneurship. In J. Brewer & S. W. Gibson (Eds.), *Institutional case studies on necessity entrepreneurship* (pp. 195–226). Cheltenham, UK: Edward Elgar Publishing Inc.

Webster, M., & Sell, J. (2014). Why do experiments? In M. Webster & J. Sell (Eds.), *Laboratory experiments in the social sciences* (pp. 5–23). Burlington, MA: Academic Press.

Weigmann, K. (2013). Educating the brain. *EMBO Reports, 14*(2), 136–139.

Weijer, C., Bruni, T., Gofton, T., Young, G. B., Norton, L., Peterson, A., & Owen, A. M. (2016). Ethical considerations in functional magnetic resonance imaging research in acutely comatose patients. *Brain, 139*(1), 292–299.

Welpe, I. M., Spörrle, M., Grichnik, D., Michl, T., & Audretsch, D. B. (2012). Emotions and opportunities: The interplay of opportunity evaluation, fear, joy, and anger as antecedent of entrepreneurial exploitation. *Entrepreneurship Theory and Practice*, *36*, 69–96.

Wiklund, J., Hatak, I., Lerner, D. A., Verheul, I., Thurik, R., & Antshel, K. (2020). Entrepreneurship, clinical psychology, and mental health: An exciting and promising new field of research. *Academy of Management Perspectives*, *34*(2), 291–295.

Wiklund, J., Nikolaev, B., Shir, N., Foo, M.-D., & Bradley, S. (2019). Entrepreneurship and well-being: Past, present, and future. *Journal of Business Venturing*, *34*(4), 579–588.

Wiklund, J., Patzelt, H., & Dimov, D. (2016). Entrepreneurship and psychological disorders: How ADHD can be productively harnessed. *Journal of Business Venturing Insights*, *6*, 14–20.

Williams, D. W., Wood, M. S., Mitchell, J. R., & Urbig, D. (2019). Applying experimental methods to advance entrepreneurship research: On the need for and publication of experiments. *Journal of Business Venturing*, *34*(2), 215–223.

Wilson, T. D., Aronson, E., & Carlsmith, K. (2010). The art of laboratory experimentation. In S. T. Fiske, D. T. Gilbert, & G. Lindzey (Eds.), *Handbook of social psychology* (5th ed., Vol. 1, pp. 51–88). Hoboken, NJ: John Wiley & Sons Inc.

Wolf, S. M., Lawrenz, F. P., Nelson, C. A., Kahn, J. P., Cho, M. K., Clayton, E. W., . . . Hudson, K. (2008). Managing incidental findings in human subjects research: Analysis and recommendations. *The Journal of Law, Medicine & Ethics*, *36*(2), 219–248.

Woodman, G. F. (2010). A brief introduction to the use of event-related potentials in studies of perception and attention. *Attention, Perception, & Psychophysics*, *72*(8), 2031–2046.

Yarkoni, T., & Braver, T. S. (2010). Cognitive neuroscience approaches to individual differences in working memory and executive control: Conceptual and methodological issues. In A. Gruszka, G. Matthews, & B. Szymura (Eds.), *Handbook of individual differences in cognition: Attention, memory and executive control* (pp. 87–108). New York, NY: Springer.

Yin, H. H., Mulcare, S. P., Hilário, M. R., Clouse, E., Holloway, T., Davis, M. I., . . . Costa, R. M. (2009). Dynamic reorganization of striatal circuits during the acquisition and consolidation of a skill. *Nature Neuroscience*, *12*(3), 333–341.

Zahra, S. A. (2007). Contextualizing theory building in entrepreneurship research. *Journal of Business Venturing*, *22*(3), 443–452.

Zampetakis, L. A., Lerakis, M., Kafetsios, K., & Moustakis, V. (2015). Investigating the emotional impact of entrepreneurship programs. *Journal of Business Venturing Insights*, *4*, 38–41.

Zani, A., Biella, G., & Proverbio, A. M. (2003). Brain imaging techniques: Invasiveness and spatial and temporal resolution. In A. Zani & A. M. Proverbio (Eds.), *The cognitive electrophysiology of mind and brain* (pp. 417–422). San Diego, CA: Academic Press.

Zaro, M. A., da Cruz Fagundes, L., Rocha, F. T., & Nunes, W. C. (2016). Cognitive brain mapping used in the study of entrepreneurial behavior – pilot test with the use of Electroencephalogram – EEG during the process of identification of business opportunities. *American Journal of Educational Research*, *4*(6), 472–478.

Zhu, J. (2004). Locating volition. *Consciousness and Cognition, 13*(2), 302–322.

Zhu, Y. (2015). The role of Qing (positive emotions) and Li 1 (rationality) in Chinese entrepreneurial decision making: A Confucian Ren-Yi Wisdom perspective. *Journal of Business Ethics, 126,* 613–630.

Zinke, K., Zeintl, M., Rose, N. S., Putzmann, J., Pydde, A., & Kliegel, M. (2014). Working memory training and transfer in older adults: Effects of age, baseline performance, and training gains. *Developmental Psychology, 50*(1), 304.

Index

Note: Page numbers in *italics* indicate a figure and page numbers in **bold** indicate a table on the corresponding page.

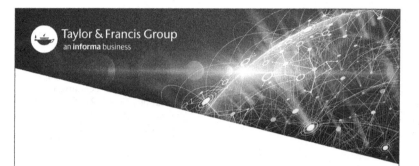

Printed in the United States
by Baker & Taylor Publisher Services